A LIVING HOPE: THE GOSPEL OF JESUS CHRIST ILLUSTRATED
Copyright © 2020 by Dominic Fam
All illustrations Copyright © 2020 by Dominic Fam

Scripture taken from the King James Version.
Editorial liberties were taken with the punctuation for easier reading.
Although this book contains excerpts from the Gospels according to Matthew, Mark, Luke and John, it does not contain the full text of the four Gospels and is therefore intended only as a companion to the full text found in the Holy Scriptures.

First Edition: 2021

Book design and illustrations by Dominic Fam

ISBN 978-981-14-8034-8 (paperback)
ISBN 978-981-14-8041-6 (ebook)

Published by DOMINIQUE FAM ILLUSTRATIONS
dominiquefam.com/alivinghope

# Contents

*He left His Father's throne above, So free, so infinite His grace;*
*Emptied Himself of all but love, And bled for Adam's helpless race;*
*'Tis mercy all, immense and free; For, O my God, it found out me.*
*("And Can It Be" by Charles Wesley, 1738)*

# Introduction

Years ago, I was reading Exodus 14 when verse 21 seemed to leap out at me. Even though I had read the book of Exodus many times before, I had always pictured this scene taking place under fairly well-lit conditions and not in the dark of night, probably due to the movies and paintings I had been used to seeing since I was a kid.

But the image of Israel crossing the Red Sea by night kept tugging at me. So one day, I decided to do an illustration based on my revised understanding. The first thing I did was gather all the text from the different books of Scripture concerning the parting of the Red Sea, to create a framework of information within which I would try to recreate the scene. I was experimenting with a hyperrealistic style at the time, and the result was the illustration on the left.

Once I had finished, however, I started to wonder if I could create other scenes using the same process. One of the things that has always nagged at me (especially during Christmas time) was the conflation of elements in Luke 2:8–20 and Matthew 2:1–23 in order to create a singular nativity scene in paintings and sculptures. So I decided to do four separate illustrations to portray the events and timeline more accurately.

I began to do the same with other Gospel accounts. At first, I had only intended to explore certain narratives through my illustrations, such as the many miracles performed by Jesus, the often debated anointing accounts, and the differences between the two cleansings of the temple. But as I went along, I started to develop ideas for more and more scenes. And as the years went by, I found myself with a growing collection of illustrations centred around the life, ministry, death and resurrection of Jesus Christ.

The scenes that held special significance to me were those leading up to the crucifixion. In particular, I wanted to represent the sufferings of Christ in a way that was more congruent with an understanding of ancient practices. An example of this are the wounds of Jesus. Having grown up in a very traditional church environment, I was used to seeing paintings and sculptures of Jesus showing a gash at His side as He hung on the cross. In reality, Jesus suffered a great deal more. He was bound, was beaten, was stripped, was scourged by multi-thonged whips that were designed to rip off chunks of flesh, had a crown of thorns pressed onto His head, was beaten with a staff, had His beard torn off, was made to carry a heavy crossbeam, was nailed to the cross for six hours, and was pierced at the side with a spear, among other punishments. Isaiah 53:5 tells us that "he was wounded for our transgressions, he was bruised for our iniquities: the chastisement of our peace was upon him; and with his stripes we are healed." These are the sufferings that the Lord Jesus willingly went through for you and me, and this demonstrates the extent of God's love for us (1 John 4:10). I wanted to portray these scenes in detail.

The resurrection is, of course, the central claim of the Christian faith, since it is through the resurrection of Jesus Christ that we are born again to a living hope (1 Peter 1:3). So it was important to me to attempt to represent as many of the post-resurrection appearances of Jesus as I could. I must note that the depiction of the locale of 1 Corinthians 15:6 is largely speculation on my part due to the scant information available. I have, however, left out the appearances in 1 Corinthians 15:5 and 1 Corinthians 15:7. These seemed to have been private appearances to Peter and James (unlike the public appearance in 1 Corinthians 15:6), so I thought it best not to speculate on those meetings.

Naturally, it would be an unrealistic goal for me to truly express the majesty, beauty and perfection of the Lord Jesus and His acts through my artwork. My intention and hope is to create artwork that faithfully depicts events as they are described in the Word of God. This book is a collection of those illustrations.

---

*And Moses stretched out his hand over the sea; and the Lord caused the sea to go back by a strong east wind all that night, and made the sea dry land, and the waters were divided.*
*(Exodus 14:21)*

NOT BY MIGHT, NOR BY POWER, BUT BY MY SPIRIT. (ZC 4:6) I SOUGHT THE LORD, AND HE HEARD ME, AND DELIVERED ME FROM ALL MY FEARS. (PS 34:4) FOR WITH GOD NOTHING SHALL BE IMPOSSIBLE. (LK 1:37) FEAR YE NOT, STAND STILL, AND SEE THE SALVATION OF THE LORD. (EX 14:13) O GIVE THANKS UNTO THE LORD; FOR HE IS GOOD: BECAUSE HIS MERCY ENDURETH FOR EVER. (PS 118:1) AND THE LORD, HE IT IS THAT DOTH GO BEFORE THEE; HE WILL BE WITH THEE, HE WILL NOT FAIL THEE, NEITHER FORSAKE THEE: FEAR NOT, NEITHER BE DISMAYED. (DE 31:8) LET NOT YOUR HEART BE TROUBLED: YE BELIEVE IN GOD, BELIEVE ALSO IN ME. (JN 14:1) TRUST IN THE LORD WITH ALL THINE HEART; AND LEAN NOT UNTO THINE OWN UNDERSTANDING. IN ALL THY WAYS ACKNOWLEDGE HIM, AND HE SHALL DIRECT THY PATHS. (PR 3:5–6) SURELY GOODNESS AND MERCY SHALL FOLLOW ME ALL THE DAYS OF MY LIFE: AND I WILL DWELL IN THE HOUSE OF THE LORD FOR EVER. (PS 23:6) ARISE, SHINE; FOR THY LIGHT IS COME, AND THE GLORY OF THE LORD IS RISEN UPON THEE. (IS 60:1) BECAUSE HE HATH SET HIS LOVE UPON ME, THEREFORE WILL I DELIVER HIM: I WILL SET HIM ON HIGH, BECAUSE HE HATH KNOWN MY NAME. HE SHALL CALL UPON ME, AND I WILL ANSWER HIM: I WILL BE WITH HIM IN TROUBLE; I WILL DELIVER HIM, AND HONOUR HIM. (PS 91:14–15) THE HOPE OF THE RIGHTEOUS SHALL BE GLADNESS: BUT THE EXPECTATION OF THE WICKED SHALL PERISH. (PR 10:28) FOR GOD HATH NOT GIVEN US THE SPIRIT OF FEAR; BUT OF POWER, AND OF LOVE, AND OF A SOUND MIND. (2 TIM 1:7) BLESSED IS HE WHOSE TRANSGRESSION IS FORGIVEN, WHOSE SIN IS COVERED. (PS 32:1) THOU WILT KEEP HIM IN PERFECT PEACE, WHOSE MIND IS STAYED ON THEE: BECAUSE HE TRUSTETH IN THEE. TRUST YE IN THE LORD FOR EVER: FOR IN THE LORD JEHOVAH IS EVERLASTING STRENGTH. (IS 26:3–4) NOW THE LORD IS THAT SPIRIT: AND WHERE THE SPIRIT OF THE LORD IS, THERE IS LIBERTY. (2 CO 3:17) THOU ART MY GOD, AND I WILL PRAISE THEE: THOU ART MY GOD, I WILL EXALT THEE. (PS 118:28) BE CAREFUL FOR NOTHING; BUT IN EVERY THING BY PRAYER AND SUPPLICATION WITH THANKSGIVING LET YOUR REQUESTS BE MADE KNOWN UNTO GOD. AND THE PEACE OF GOD, WHICH PASSETH ALL UNDERSTANDING, SHALL KEEP YOUR HEARTS AND MINDS THROUGH CHRIST JESUS. (PP 4:6–7) FOR IN HIM WE LIVE, AND MOVE, AND HAVE OUR BEING. (ACTS 17:28) CAST THY BURDEN UPON THE LORD, AND HE SHALL SUSTAIN THEE: HE SHALL NEVER SUFFER THE RIGHTEOUS TO BE MOVED. (PS 55:22) NO WEAPON THAT IS FORMED AGAINST THEE SHALL PROSPER; AND EVERY TONGUE THAT SHALL RISE AGAINST THEE IN JUDGMENT THOU SHALT CONDEMN. THIS IS THE HERITAGE OF THE SERVANTS OF THE LORD, AND THEIR RIGHTEOUSNESS IS OF ME, SAITH THE LORD. (IS 54:17) THE EFFECTUAL FERVENT PRAYER OF A RIGHTEOUS MAN AVAILETH MUCH. (JM 5:16) SO TEACH US TO NUMBER OUR DAYS, THAT WE MAY APPLY OUR HEARTS UNTO WISDOM. (PS 90:12) FOR THE JOY OF THE LORD IS YOUR STRENGTH. (NE 8:10) HE THAT DWELLETH IN THE SECRET PLACE OF THE MOST HIGH SHALL ABIDE UNDER THE SHADOW OF THE ALMIGHTY. I WILL SAY OF THE LORD, HE IS MY REFUGE AND MY FORTRESS: MY GOD; IN HIM WILL I TRUST. (PS 91:1–2) O MY GOD, I TRUST IN THEE: LET ME NOT BE ASHAMED, LET NOT MINE ENEMIES TRIUMPH OVER ME. (PS 25:2) BEFORE I FORMED THEE IN THE BELLY I KNEW THEE; AND BEFORE THOU CAMEST FORTH OUT OF THE WOMB I SANCTIFIED THEE, AND I ORDAINED THEE A PROPHET UNTO THE NATIONS. (JE 1:5) FOR I WILL BE MERCIFUL TO THEIR UNRIGHTEOUSNESS, AND THEIR SINS AND THEIR INIQUITIES WILL I REMEMBER NO MORE. (HE 8:12) IT IS OF THE LORD'S MERCIES THAT WE ARE NOT CONSUMED, BECAUSE HIS COMPASSIONS FAIL NOT. (LA 3:22) AND I WILL REBUKE THE DEVOURER FOR YOUR SAKES, AND HE SHALL NOT DESTROY THE FRUITS OF YOUR GROUND; NEITHER SHALL YOUR VINE CAST HER FRUIT BEFORE THE TIME IN THE FIELD, SAITH THE LORD OF HOSTS. (MAL 3:11) HEREBY KNOW YE THE SPIRIT OF GOD: EVERY SPIRIT THAT CONFESSETH THAT JESUS CHRIST IS COME IN THE FLESH IS OF GOD. (1 JN 4:2) HITHERTO HATH THE LORD HELPED US. (1 SAM 7:12) FOR WHOSOEVER SHALL CALL UPON THE NAME OF THE LORD SHALL BE SAVED. (RM 10:13) LET EVERY THING THAT HATH BREATH PRAISE THE LORD. PRAISE YE THE LORD. (PS 150:6) THE LORD IS GOOD, A STRONG HOLD IN THE DAY OF TROUBLE; AND HE KNOWETH THEM THAT TRUST IN HIM. (NA 1:7) NOW FAITH IS THE SUBSTANCE OF THINGS HOPED FOR, THE EVIDENCE OF THINGS NOT SEEN. (HE 11:1) BUT THEY THAT WAIT UPON THE LORD SHALL RENEW THEIR STRENGTH; THEY SHALL MOUNT UP WITH WINGS AS EAGLES; THEY SHALL RUN, AND NOT BE WEARY; AND THEY SHALL WALK, AND NOT FAINT. (IS 40:31) FOR I KNOW THE THOUGHTS THAT I THINK TOWARD YOU, SAITH THE LORD, THOUGHTS OF PEACE, AND NOT OF EVIL, TO GIVE YOU AN EXPECTED END. (JE 29:11) FOR AS THE BODY WITHOUT THE SPIRIT IS DEAD, SO FAITH WITHOUT WORKS IS DEAD ALSO. (JM 2:26) HE WHICH HATH BEGUN A GOOD WORK IN YOU WILL PERFORM IT UNTIL THE DAY OF JESUS CHRIST. (PHIL 1:6) THE LORD IS MY SHEPHERD; I SHALL NOT WANT. (PS 23:1) AND YE SHALL SERVE THE LORD YOUR GOD, AND HE SHALL BLESS THY BREAD, AND THY WATER; AND I WILL TAKE SICKNESS AWAY FROM THE MIDST OF THEE. (EX 23:25) YEA, AND ALL THAT WILL LIVE GODLY IN CHRIST JESUS SHALL SUFFER PERSECUTION. (2 TI 3:12) GREATER IS HE THAT IS IN YOU, THAN HE THAT IS IN THE WORLD. (1 JN 4:4) AND HOPE MAKETH NOT ASHAMED; BECAUSE THE LOVE OF GOD IS SHED ABROAD IN OUR HEARTS BY THE HOLY GHOST WHICH IS GIVEN UNTO US. (RM 5:5) I WILL INSTRUCT THEE AND TEACH THEE IN THE WAY WHICH THOU SHALT GO: I WILL GUIDE THEE WITH MINE EYE. (PS 32:8) AND HE SAID, MY PRESENCE SHALL GO WITH THEE, AND I WILL GIVE THEE REST. (EX 33:14) WITH GOD ALL THINGS ARE POSSIBLE. (MT 19:26) HE THAT SPARED NOT HIS OWN SON, BUT DELIVERED HIM UP FOR US ALL, HOW SHALL HE NOT WITH HIM ALSO FREELY GIVE US ALL THINGS? (RM 8:32) HEREIN IS LOVE, NOT THAT WE LOVED GOD, BUT THAT HE LOVED US, AND SENT HIS SON TO BE THE PROPITIATION FOR OUR SINS. (1 JN 4:10) FOR I WILL RESTORE HEALTH UNTO THEE, AND I WILL HEAL THEE OF THY WOUNDS, SAITH THE LORD; BECAUSE THEY CALLED THEE AN OUTCAST, SAYING, THIS IS ZION, WHOM NO MAN SEEKETH AFTER. (JE 30:17) FOR THE MOUNTAINS SHALL DEPART, AND THE HILLS BE REMOVED; BUT MY KINDNESS SHALL NOT DEPART FROM THEE, NEITHER SHALL THE COVENANT OF MY PEACE BE REMOVED, SAITH THE LORD THAT HATH MERCY ON THEE. (IS 54:10) THEREFORE IT IS OF FAITH, THAT IT MIGHT BE BY GRACE; TO THE END THE PROMISE MIGHT BE SURE TO ALL THE SEED. (RM 4:16) BUT THE PATH OF THE JUST IS AS THE SHINING LIGHT, THAT SHINETH MORE AND MORE UNTO THE PERFECT DAY. (PR 4:18) BUT BE YE DOERS OF THE WORD, AND NOT HEARERS ONLY, DECEIVING YOUR OWN SELVES. (JM 1:22) THE LORD IS MY STRENGTH AND SONG, AND HE IS BECOME MY SALVATION: HE IS MY GOD, AND I WILL PREPARE HIM AN HABITATION; MY FATHER'S GOD, AND I WILL EXALT HIM. (EX 15:2) IN THE DAY WHEN I CRIED THOU ANSWEREDST ME, AND STRENGTHENEDST ME WITH STRENGTH IN MY SOUL. (PS 138:3) LET US THEREFORE COME BOLDLY UNTO THE THRONE OF GRACE, THAT WE MAY OBTAIN MERCY, AND FIND GRACE TO HELP IN TIME OF NEED. (HE 4:16) FOR BY GRACE ARE YE SAVED THROUGH FAITH; AND THAT NOT OF YOURSELVES: IT IS THE GIFT OF GOD. (EPH 2:8) HUMBLE YOURSELVES THEREFORE UNDER THE MIGHTY HAND OF GOD, THAT HE MAY EXALT YOU IN DUE TIME: CASTING ALL YOUR CARE UPON HIM; FOR HE CARETH FOR YOU. (1 PET 5:6–7) BUT GODLINESS WITH CONTENTMENT IS GREAT GAIN. (1 TI 6:6) COME UNTO ME, ALL YE THAT LABOUR AND ARE HEAVY LADEN, AND I WILL GIVE YOU REST. (MT 11:28) IN EVERY THING GIVE THANKS: FOR THIS IS THE WILL OF GOD IN CHRIST JESUS CONCERNING YOU. (1 TH 5:18) AND YE SHALL SEEK ME, AND FIND ME, WHEN YE SHALL SEARCH FOR ME WITH ALL YOUR HEART. (JE 29:13) FEAR THOU NOT; FOR I AM WITH THEE: BE NOT DISMAYED; FOR I AM THY GOD: I WILL STRENGTHEN THEE; YEA, I WILL HELP THEE; YEA, I WILL UPHOLD THEE WITH THE RIGHT HAND OF MY RIGHTEOUSNESS. (IS 41:10) WHO IS HE THAT OVERCOMETH THE WORLD, BUT HE THAT BELIEVETH THAT JESUS IS THE SON OF GOD? (1 JN 5:5) AND HE SAID UNTO ME, MY GRACE IS SUFFICIENT FOR THEE: FOR MY STRENGTH IS MADE PERFECT IN WEAKNESS. MOST GLADLY THEREFORE WILL I RATHER GLORY IN MY INFIRMITIES, THAT THE POWER OF CHRIST MAY REST UPON ME. (2 CO 12:9) SO SHALL MY WORD BE THAT GOETH FORTH OUT OF MY MOUTH: IT SHALL NOT RETURN UNTO ME VOID, BUT IT SHALL ACCOMPLISH THAT WHICH I PLEASE, AND IT SHALL PROSPER IN THE THING WHERETO I SENT IT. (IS 55:11) AS ONE WHOM HIS MOTHER COMFORTETH, SO WILL I COMFORT YOU; AND YE SHALL BE COMFORTED IN JERUSALEM. (IS 66:13) THE LORD IS MY LIGHT AND MY SALVATION; WHOM SHALL I FEAR? THE LORD IS THE STRENGTH OF MY LIFE; OF WHOM SHALL I BE AFRAID? (PS 27:1) BUT NOW IN CHRIST JESUS YE WHO SOMETIMES WERE FAR OFF ARE MADE NIGH BY THE BLOOD OF CHRIST. (EPH 2:13) FOR ALL THE PROMISES OF GOD IN HIM ARE YEA, AND IN HIM AMEN, UNTO THE GLORY OF GOD BY US. (2 CO 1:20) HE THAT IS OUR GOD IS THE GOD OF SALVATION; AND UNTO GOD THE LORD BELONG THE ISSUES FROM DEATH. (PS 68:20) JESUS CHRIST THE SAME YESTERDAY, AND TO DAY, AND FOR EVER. (HE 13:8) AS IT IS WRITTEN, THE JUST SHALL LIVE BY FAITH. (RM 1:17) HEAL ME, O LORD, AND I SHALL BE HEALED; SAVE ME, AND I SHALL BE SAVED: FOR THOU ART MY PRAISE. (JE 17:14) FOR WE WALK BY FAITH, NOT BY SIGHT. (2 CO 5:7) THE HEAVENS DECLARE HIS RIGHTEOUSNESS, AND ALL THE PEOPLE SEE HIS GLORY. (PS 97:6) THE LORD BLESS THEE, AND KEEP THEE: THE LORD MAKE HIS FACE SHINE UPON THEE, AND BE GRACIOUS UNTO THEE: THE LORD LIFT UP HIS COUNTENANCE UPON THEE, AND GIVE THEE PEACE. (NM 6:24–26)

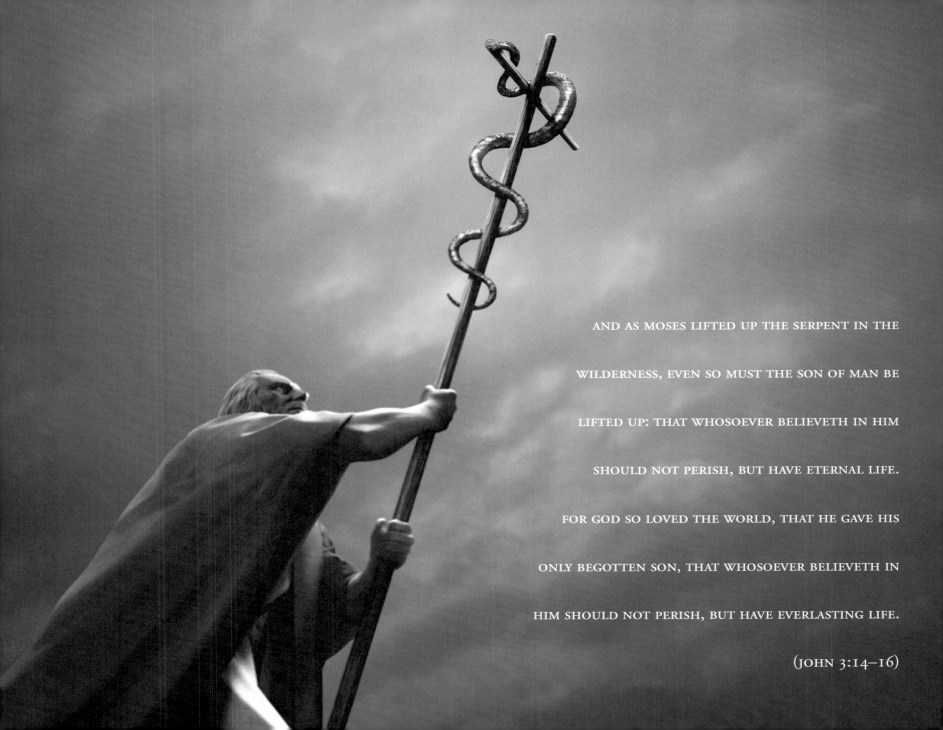

AND AS MOSES LIFTED UP THE SERPENT IN THE

WILDERNESS, EVEN SO MUST THE SON OF MAN BE

LIFTED UP: THAT WHOSOEVER BELIEVETH IN HIM

SHOULD NOT PERISH, BUT HAVE ETERNAL LIFE.

FOR GOD SO LOVED THE WORLD, THAT HE GAVE HIS

ONLY BEGOTTEN SON, THAT WHOSOEVER BELIEVETH IN

HIM SHOULD NOT PERISH, BUT HAVE EVERLASTING LIFE.

(JOHN 3:14–16)

BUT HE WAS WOUNDED FOR OUR TRANSGRESSIONS,

HE WAS BRUISED FOR OUR INIQUITIES:

THE CHASTISEMENT OF OUR PEACE WAS UPON HIM;

AND WITH HIS STRIPES WE ARE HEALED.

(ISAIAH 53:5)

# In the beginning was the Word

In the beginning was the Word, and the Word was with God, and the Word was God. The same was in the beginning with God. All things were made by him; and without him was not any thing made that was made. In him was life; and the life was the light of men. And the light shineth in darkness; and the darkness comprehended it not.

There was a man sent from God, whose name was John. The same came for a witness, to bear witness of the Light, that all men through him might believe. He was not that Light, but was sent to bear witness of that Light. That was the true Light, which lighteth every man that cometh into the world.

He was in the world, and the world was made by him, and the world knew him not. He came unto his own, and his own received him not. But as many as received him, to them gave he power to become the sons of God, even to them that believe on his name: Which were born, not of blood, nor of the will of the flesh, nor of the will of man, but of God.

And the Word was made flesh, and dwelt among us, (and we beheld his glory, the glory as of the only begotten of the Father,) full of grace and truth.

John bare witness of him, and cried, saying, This was he of whom I spake, He that cometh after me is preferred before me: for he was before me.

And of his fulness have all we received, and grace for grace. For the law was given by Moses, but grace and truth came by Jesus Christ. No man hath seen God at any time, the only begotten Son, which is in the bosom of the Father, he hath declared him.
(John 1:1–18)

*In the beginning God created the heaven and the earth.*
*(Genesis 1:1)*

# This shall be a sign unto you

And there were in the same country shepherds abiding in the field, keeping watch over their flock by night. And, lo, the angel of the Lord came upon them, and the glory of the Lord shone round about them: and they were sore afraid. And the angel said unto them, Fear not: for, behold, I bring you good tidings of great joy, which shall be to all people. For unto you is born this day in the city of David a Saviour, which is Christ the Lord. And this shall be a sign unto you; Ye shall find the babe wrapped in swaddling clothes, lying in a manger.

And suddenly there was with the angel a multitude of the heavenly host praising God, and saying,
　　Glory to God in the highest, and on earth peace, good will toward men.
(Luke 2:8–14)

*For unto us a child is born, unto us a son is given: and the government shall be upon his shoulder: and his name shall be called Wonderful, Counsellor, The mighty God, The everlasting Father, The Prince of Peace. Of the increase of his government and peace there shall be no end, upon the throne of David, and upon his kingdom, to order it, and to establish it with judgment and with justice from henceforth even for ever. The zeal of the Lord of hosts will perform this.*
*(Isaiah 9:6–7)*

# The Babe lying in a manger

And it came to pass, as the angels were gone away from them into heaven, the shepherds said one to another, Let us now go even unto Bethlehem, and see this thing which is come to pass, which the Lord hath made known unto us. And they came with haste, and found Mary, and Joseph, and the babe lying in a manger. And when they had seen it, they made known abroad the saying which was told them concerning this child. And all they that heard it wondered at those things which were told them by the shepherds. But Mary kept all these things, and pondered them in her heart. And the shepherds returned, glorifying and praising God for all the things that they had heard and seen, as it was told unto them. (Luke 2:15–20)

*Therefore the Lord himself shall give you a sign; Behold, a virgin shall conceive, and bear a son, and shall call his name Immanuel.*
*(Isaiah 7:14)*

THE KING OF KINGS LAY THUS IN LOWLY MANGER; IN ALL OUR TRIALS BORN TO BE OUR FRIEND

Now the birth of Jesus Christ was
this wise: When as his mother M
was espoused to Joseph, before th
came together, she was found w
child of the Holy Ghost. Then Jos
her husband, being a just man, and
willing to make her a public exam
was minded to put her away priv
But while he thought on these thir
behold, the angel of the Lord appe
unto him in a dream, saying, Jose
thou son of David, fear not to ta
unto thee Mary thy wife: for th
which is conceived in her is
of the Holy Ghost.

(Matthew 1:18-20)

# Mine eyes have seen Thy salvation

And when the days of her purification according to the law of Moses were accomplished, they brought him to Jerusalem, to present him to the Lord; (As it is written in the law of the Lord, Every male that openeth the womb shall be called holy to the Lord; And to offer a sacrifice according to that which is said in the law of the Lord, A pair of turtledoves, or two young pigeons.

And, behold, there was a man in Jerusalem, whose name was Simeon; and the same man was just and devout, waiting for the consolation of Israel: and the Holy Ghost was upon him. And it was revealed unto him by the Holy Ghost, that he should not see death, before he had seen the Lord's Christ. And he came by the Spirit into the temple: and when the parents brought in the child Jesus, to do for him after the custom of the law, Then took he him up in his arms, and blessed God, and said,

Lord, now lettest thou thy servant depart in peace,
according to thy word: For mine eyes have seen thy salvation,
Which thou hast prepared before the face of all people;
A light to lighten the Gentiles,
and the glory of thy people Israel.

And Joseph and his mother marvelled at those things which were spoken of him. And Simeon blessed them, and said unto Mary his mother, Behold, this child is set for the fall and rising again of many in Israel; and for a sign which shall be spoken against; (Yea, a sword shall pierce through thy own soul also,) that the thoughts of many hearts may be revealed.

And there was one Anna, a prophetess, the daughter of Phanuel, of the tribe of Aser: she was of a great age, and had lived with an husband seven years from her virginity; And she was a widow of about fourscore and four years, which departed not from the temple, but served God with fastings and prayers night and day. And she coming in that instant gave thanks likewise unto the Lord, and spake of him to all them that looked for redemption in Jerusalem.

And when they had performed all things according to the law of the Lord, they returned into Galilee, to their own city Nazareth. And the child grew, and waxed strong in spirit, filled with wisdom: and the grace of God was upon him.
(Luke 2:22–40)

---

*And the Lord spake unto Moses, saying, Sanctify unto me all the firstborn, whatsoever openeth the womb among the children of Israel, both of man and of beast: it is mine.*
*(Exodus 13:1–2)*

# Wise men from the east

Now when Jesus was born in Bethlehem of Judaea in the days of Herod the king, behold, there came wise men from the east to Jerusalem, Saying, Where is he that is born King of the Jews? for we have seen his star in the east, and are come to worship him.

When Herod the king had heard these things, he was troubled, and all Jerusalem with him. And when he had gathered all the chief priests and scribes of the people together, he demanded of them where Christ should be born.

And they said unto him, In Bethlehem of Judaea: for thus it is written by the prophet,
And thou Bethlehem, in the land of Juda, art not the least among the princes of Juda: for out of thee shall come a Governor, that shall rule my people Israel.
(Matthew 2:1–6)

---

*So all the generations from Abraham to David are fourteen generations; and from David until the carrying away into Babylon are fourteen generations; and from the carrying away into Babylon unto Christ are fourteen generations.*
*(Matthew 1:17)*

But thou, Bethlehem Ephratah, though thou be little among the thousands of Judah, yet out of thee shall he come forth unto me that is to be ruler in Israel; whose goings forth have been from of old, from everlasting.

(Micah 5:2)

# They presented unto Him gifts

Then Herod, when he had privily called the wise men, enquired of them diligently what time the star appeared. And he sent them to Bethlehem, and said, Go and search diligently for the young child; and when ye have found him, bring me word again, that I may come and worship him also.

When they had heard the king, they departed; and, lo, the star, which they saw in the east, went before them, till it came and stood over where the young child was. When they saw the star, they rejoiced with exceeding great joy. And when they were come into the house, they saw the young child with Mary his mother, and fell down, and worshipped him: and when they had opened their treasures, they presented unto him gifts; gold, and frankincense and myrrh.

And being warned of God in a dream that they should not return to Herod, they departed into their own country another way.

And when they were departed, behold, the angel of the Lord appeareth to Joseph in a dream, saying, Arise, and take the young child and his mother, and flee into Egypt, and be thou there until I bring thee word: for Herod will seek the young child to destroy him.

When he arose, he took the young child and his mother by night, and departed into Egypt: And was there until the death of Herod: that it might be fulfilled which was spoken of the Lord by the prophet, saying, Out of Egypt have I called my son.

Then Herod, when he saw that he was mocked of the wise men, was exceeding wroth, and sent forth, and slew all the children that were in Bethlehem, and in all the coasts thereof, from two years old and under, according to the time which he had diligently inquired of the wise men. Then was fulfilled that which was spoken by Jeremiah the prophet, saying,

In Rama was there a voice heard, lamentation, and weeping, and great mourning, Rachel weeping for her children, and would not be comforted, because they are not.

But when Herod was dead, behold, an angel of the Lord appeareth in a dream to Joseph in Egypt, Saying, Arise, and take the young child and his mother, and go into the land of Israel: for they are dead which sought the young child's life. And he arose, and took the young child and his mother, and came into the land of Israel.

But when he heard that Archelaus did reign in Judaea in the room of his father Herod, he was afraid to go thither: notwithstanding, being warned of God in a dream, he turned aside into the parts of Galilee: And he came and dwelt in a city called Nazareth: that it might be fulfilled which was spoken by the prophets, He shall be called a Nazarene. (Matthew 2:7–23)

---

*Let this mind be in you, which was also in Christ Jesus: Who, being in the form of God, thought it not robbery to be equal with God: But made himself of no reputation, and took upon him the form of a servant, and was made in the likeness of men. (Philippians 2:5–7)*

And the angel said unto her, Fear not, Mary: for thou hast found favour with God. And, behold, thou shalt conceive in thy womb, and bring forth a son, and shalt call his name Jesus. He shall be great, and shall be called the Son of the Highest: and the Lord God shall give unto him the throne of his father David: And he shall reign over the house of Jacob for ever; and of his kingdom there shall be no end.

(Luke 1:30-33)

# My Father's business

Now his parents went to Jerusalem every year at the feast of the passover. And when he was twelve years old, they went up to Jerusalem after the custom of the feast. And when they had fulfilled the days, as they returned, the child Jesus tarried behind in Jerusalem; and Joseph and his mother knew not of it. But they, supposing him to have been in the company, went a day's journey; and they sought him among their kinsfolk and acquaintance. And when they found him not, they turned back again to Jerusalem, seeking him. And it came to pass, that after three days they found him in the temple, sitting in the midst of the doctors, both hearing them, and asking them questions. And all that heard him were astonished at his understanding and answers. And when they saw him, they were amazed: and his mother said unto him, Son, why hast thou thus dealt with us? behold, thy father and I have sought thee sorrowing.

And he said unto them, How is it that ye sought me? wist ye not that I must be about my Father's business? And they understood not the saying which he spake unto them. And he went down with them, and came to Nazareth, and was subject unto them: but his mother kept all these sayings in her heart.

And Jesus increased in wisdom and stature, and in favour with God and man.
(Luke 2:41–52)

---

*For Moses truly said unto the fathers, A prophet shall the Lord your God raise up unto you of your brethren, like unto me; him shall ye hear in all things whatsoever he shall say unto you.*
*(Acts 3:22)*

And there shall come forth a rod out of the stem of Jesse, and a Branch shall grow out of his roots: And the spirit of the Lord shall rest upon him, the spirit of wisdom and understanding, the spirit of counsel and might, the spirit of knowledge and of the fear of the Lord.

(Isaiah 11:1–2)

# In whom I am well pleased

In those days came John the Baptist, preaching in the wilderness of Judaea, And saying, Repent ye: for the kingdom of heaven is at hand. For this is he that was spoken of by the prophet Esaias, saying,

The voice of one crying in the wilderness,
Prepare ye the way of the Lord,
make his paths straight.

And the same John had his raiment of camel's hair, and a leathern girdle about his loins; and his meat was locusts and wild honey.

Then went out to him Jerusalem, and all Judaea, and all the region round about Jordan, And were baptized of him in Jordan, confessing their sins. But when he saw many of the Pharisees and Sadducees come to his baptism, he said unto them, O generation of vipers, who hath warned you to flee from the wrath to come? Bring forth therefore fruits meet for repentance: And think not to say within yourselves, We have Abraham to our father: for I say unto you, that God is able of these stones to raise up children unto Abraham. And now also the axe is laid unto the root of the trees: therefore every tree which bringeth not forth good fruit is hewn down, and cast into the fire. I indeed baptize you with water unto repentance. but he that cometh after me is mightier than I, whose shoes I am not worthy to bear: he shall baptize you with the Holy Ghost, and with fire: Whose fan is in his hand, and he will throughly purge his floor, and gather his wheat into the garner; but he will burn up the chaff with unquenchable fire.

Then cometh Jesus from Galilee to Jordan unto John, to be baptized of him. But John forbad him, saying, I have need to be baptized of thee, and comest thou to me?

And Jesus answering said unto him, Suffer it to be so now: for thus it becometh us to fulfil all righteousness. Then he suffered him.

And Jesus, when he was baptized, went up straightway out of the water: and, lo, the heavens were opened unto him, and he saw the Spirit of God descending like a dove, and lighting upon him: And lo a voice from heaven, saying, This is my beloved Son, in whom I am well pleased.
(Matthew 3:1–17)

*And so it is written, The first man Adam was made a living soul; the last Adam was made a quickening spirit.*
*(1 Corinthians 15:45)*

The next day John seeth Jesus coming unto him, and saith, Behold the Lamb of God, which taketh away the sin of the world. This is he of whom I said, After me cometh a man which is preferred before me: for he was before me. And I knew him not: but that he should be made manifest to Israel, therefore am I come baptizing with water. And John bare record, saying, I saw the Spirit descending from heaven like a dove, and it abode upon him. And I knew him not: but he that sent me to baptize with water, the same said unto me, Upon whom thou shalt see the Spirit descending, and remaining on him, the same is he which baptizeth with the Holy Ghost. And I saw, and bare record that this is the Son of God.

(John 1:29-34)

# Man shall not live by bread alone

And immediately the spirit driveth him into the wilderness. And he was there in the wilderness forty days, tempted of Satan; and was with the wild beasts.
(Mark 1:12–13)


And when he had fasted forty days and forty nights, he was afterward an hungred. And when the tempter came to him, he said, If thou be the Son of God, command that these stones be made bread.

But he answered and said, It is written, Man shall not live by bread alone, but by every word that proceedeth out of the mouth of God.
(Matthew 4:2–4)

---

*Now the serpent was more subtil than any beast of the field which the Lord God had made. And he said unto the woman, Yea, hath God said, Ye shall not eat of every tree of the garden? And the woman said unto the serpent, We may eat of the fruit of the trees of the garden: But of the fruit of the tree which is in the midst of the garden, God hath said, Ye shall not eat of it, neither shall ye touch it, lest ye die. And the serpent said unto the woman, Ye shall not surely die: For God doth know that in the day ye eat thereof, then your eyes shall be opened, and ye shall be as gods, knowing good and evil. And when the woman saw that the tree was good for food, and that it was pleasant to the eyes, and a tree to be desired to make one wise, she took of the fruit thereof, and did eat, and gave also unto her husband with her; and he did eat. And the eyes of them both were opened, and they knew that they were naked; and they sewed fig leaves together, and made themselves aprons.*
*(Genesis 3:1–7)*

# It is written

Then the devil taketh him up into the holy city, and setteth him on a pinnacle of the temple, And saith unto him, If thou be the Son of God, cast thyself down: for it is written,
He shall give his angels charge concerning thee:
and
in their hands they shall bear thee up,
lest at any time thou dash thy foot against a stone.

Jesus said unto him, It is written again, Thou shalt not tempt the Lord thy God. (Matthew 4:5–7)

---

*And they heard the voice of the Lord God walking in the garden in the cool of the day: and Adam and his wife hid themselves from the presence of the Lord God amongst the trees of the garden. And the Lord God called unto Adam, and said unto him, Where art thou? And he said, I heard thy voice in the garden, and I was afraid, because I was naked; and I hid myself. And he said, Who told thee that thou wast naked? Hast thou eaten of the tree, whereof I commanded thee that thou shouldest not eat? And the man said, The woman whom thou gavest to be with me, she gave me of the tree, and I did eat. And the Lord God said unto the woman, What is this that thou hast done? And the woman said, The serpent beguiled me, and I did eat. (Genesis 3:8–13)*

Blessed is the man that endureth temptation: for when he is tried, he shall receive the crown of life, which the Lord hath promised to them that love him. Let no man say when he is tempted, I am tempted of God: for God cannot be tempted with evil, neither tempteth he any man: But every man is tempted, when he is drawn away of his own lust, and enticed. Then when lust hath conceived, it bringeth forth sin: and sin, when it is finished, bringeth forth death. Do not err, my beloved brethren. Every good gift and every perfect gift is from above, and cometh down from the Father of lights, with whom is no variableness, neither shadow of turning.

(James 1:12–17)

# Him only shalt thou serve

Again, the devil taketh him up into an exceeding high mountain, and sheweth him all the kingdoms of the world, and the glory of them; And saith unto him, All these things will I give thee, if thou wilt fall down and worship me.

Then saith Jesus unto him, Get thee hence, Satan: for it is written, Thou shalt worship the Lord thy God, and him only shalt thou serve.

Then the devil leaveth him, and, behold, angels came and ministered unto him.
(Matthew 4:8–11)

---

*And the Lord God said unto the serpent, Because thou hast done this, thou art cursed above all cattle, and above every beast of the field; upon thy belly shalt thou go, and dust shalt thou eat all the days of thy life: And I will put enmity between thee and the woman, and between thy seed and her seed; it shall bruise thy head, and thou shalt bruise his heel.*
*(Genesis 3:14–15)*

# Whatsoever He saith unto you, do it

And the third day there was a marriage in Cana of Galilee; and the mother of Jesus was there: And both Jesus was called, and his disciples, to the marriage. And when they wanted wine, the mother of Jesus saith unto him, They have no wine.

Jesus saith unto her, Woman, what have I to do with thee? mine hour is not yet come.

His mother saith unto the servants, Whatsoever he saith unto you, do it.

And there were set there six waterpots of stone, after the manner of the purifying of the Jews, containing two or three firkins apiece. Jesus saith unto them, Fill the waterpots with water. And they filled them up to the brim. And he saith unto them, Draw out now, and bear unto the governor of the feast. And they bare it. When the ruler of the feast had tasted the water that was made wine, and knew not whence it was: (but the servants which drew the water knew;) the governor of the feast called the bridegroom, And saith unto him, Every man at the beginning doth set forth good wine; and when men have well drunk, then that which is worse: but thou hast kept the good wine until now.

This beginning of miracles did Jesus in Cana of Galilee, and manifested forth his glory; and his disciples believed on him. (John 2:1–11)

---

*Let us be glad and rejoice, and give honour to him: for the marriage of the Lamb is come, and his wife hath made herself ready. And to her was granted that she should be arrayed in fine linen, clean and white: for the fine linen is the righteousness of saints. And he saith unto me, Write, Blessed are they which are called unto the marriage supper of the Lamb. (Revelation 19:7–9)*

Wherefore, my brethren, ye also are become dead to the law by the body of Christ; that ye should be married to another, even to him who is raised from the dead, that we should bring forth fruit unto God. For when we were in the flesh, the motions of sins, which were by the law, did work in our members to bring forth fruit unto death. But now we are delivered from the law, that being dead wherein we were held; that we should serve in newness of spirit, and not in the oldness of the letter.

(Romans 7:4-6)

# Destroy this temple, and in three days I will raise it up

And the Jews' passover was at hand, and Jesus went up to Jerusalem. And found in the temple those that sold oxen and sheep and doves, and the changers of money sitting: And when he had made a scourge of small cords, he drove them all out of the temple, and the sheep, and the oxen; and poured out the changers' money, and overthrew the tables; And said unto them that sold doves, Take these things hence; make not my Father's house an house of merchandise. And his disciples remembered that it was written, The zeal of thine house hath eaten me up.

Then answered the Jews and said unto him, What sign shewest thou unto us, seeing that thou doest these things?

Jesus answered and said unto them, Destroy this temple, and in three days I will raise it up.

Then said the Jews, Forty and six years was this temple in building, and wilt thou rear it up in three days?

But he spake of the temple of his body. When therefore he was risen from the dead, his disciples remembered that he had said this unto them; and they believed the scripture, and the word which Jesus had said.

Now when he was in Jerusalem at the passover, in the feast day, many believed in his name, when they saw the miracles which he did. But Jesus did not commit himself unto them, because he knew all men, And needed not that any should testify of man: for he knew what was in man.
(John 2:13–25)

---

*If in this life only we have hope in Christ, we are of all men most miserable. But now is Christ risen from the dead, and become the firstfruits of them that slept. For since by man came death, by man came also the resurrection of the dead. For as in Adam all die, even so in Christ shall all be made alive.*
*(1 Corinthians 15:19–22)*

# Ye must be born again

There was a man of the Pharisees, named Nicodemus, a ruler of the Jews: The same came to Jesus by night, and said unto him, Rabbi, we know that thou art a teacher come from God: for no man can do these miracles that thou doest, except God be with him.

Jesus answered and said unto him, Verily, verily, I say unto thee, Except a man be born again, he cannot see the kingdom of God.

Nicodemus saith unto him, How can a man be born when he is old? can he enter the second time into his mother's womb, and be born?

Jesus answered, Verily, verily, I say unto thee, Except a man be born of water and of the Spirit, he cannot enter into the kingdom of God. That which is born of the flesh is flesh; and that which is born of the Spirit is spirit. Marvel not that I said unto thee, Ye must be born again. The wind bloweth where it listeth, and thou hearest the sound thereof, but canst not tell whence it cometh, and whither it goeth: so is every one that is born of the Spirit.

Nicodemus answered and said unto him, How can these things be?

Jesus answered and said unto him, Art thou a master of Israel, and knowest not these things? Verily, verily, I say unto thee, We speak that we do know, and testify that we have seen; and ye receive not our witness. If I have told you earthly things, and ye believe not, how shall ye believe, if I tell you of heavenly things? And no man hath ascended up to heaven, but he that came down from heaven, even the Son of man which is in heaven. And as Moses lifted up the serpent in the wilderness, even so must the Son of man be lifted up: That whosoever believeth in him should not perish, but have eternal life. For God so loved the world, that he gave his only begotten Son, that whosoever believeth in him should not perish, but have everlasting life. For God sent not his Son into the world to condemn the world; but that the world through him might be saved.

He that believeth on him is not condemned: but he that believeth not is condemned already, because he hath not believed in the name of the only begotten Son of God. And this is the condemnation, that light is come into the world, and men loved darkness rather than light, because their deeds were evil. For every one that doeth evil hateth the light, neither cometh to the light, lest his deeds should be reproved. But he that doeth truth cometh to the light, that his deeds may be made manifest, that they are wrought in God.
(John 3:1–21)

---

*Therefore if any man be in Christ, he is a new creature: old things are passed away; behold, all things are become new. And all things are of God, who hath reconciled us to himself by Jesus Christ, and hath given to us the ministry of reconciliation; To wit, that God was in Christ, reconciling the world unto himself, not imputing their trespasses unto them; and hath committed unto us the word of reconciliation.*
*(2 Corinthians 5:17–19)*

# Worship Him in spirit and in truth

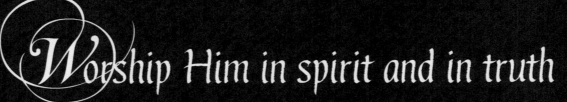

When therefore the Lord knew how the Pharisees had heard that Jesus made and baptized more disciples than John, (Though Jesus himself baptized not, but his disciples,) He left Judaea, and departed again into Galilee. And he must needs go through Samaria.

Then cometh he to a city of Samaria, which is called Sychar, near to the parcel of ground that Jacob gave to his son Joseph. Now Jacob's well was there. Jesus therefore, being wearied with his journey, sat thus on the well: and it was about the sixth hour.

There cometh a woman of Samaria to draw water: Jesus saith unto her, Give me to drink (For his disciples were gone away unto the city to buy meat.)

Then saith the woman of Samaria unto him, How is it that thou, being a Jew, askest drink of me, which am a woman of Samaria? for the Jews have no dealings with the Samaritans.

Jesus answered and said unto her, If thou knewest the gift of God, and who it is that saith to thee, Give me to drink; thou wouldest have asked of him, and he would have given thee living water. The woman saith unto him, Sir, thou hast nothing to draw with, and the well is deep: from

whence then hast thou that living water? Art thou greater than our father Jacob, which gave us the well, and drank thereof himself, and his children, and his cattle?

Jesus answered and said unto her, Whosoever drinketh of this water shall thirst again: But whosoever drinketh of the water that I shall give him shall never thirst; but the water that I shall give him shall be in him a well of water springing up into everlasting life.

The woman saith unto him, Sir, give me this water, that I thirst not, neither come hither to draw.

Jesus saith unto her, Go, call thy husband, and come hither.

The woman answered and said, I have no husband.

Jesus said unto her, Thou hast well said, I have no husband: For thou hast had five husbands; and he whom thou now hast is not thy husband: in that saidst thou truly.

The woman saith unto him, Sir, I perceive that thou art a prophet. Our fathers worshipped in this mountain; and ye say, that in Jerusalem is the place where men ought to worship.

Jesus saith unto her, Woman, believe me, the hour cometh, when ye shall neither in this mountain, nor yet at Jerusalem, worship the Father. Ye worship ye know not what: we know what we worship: for salvation is of the Jews. But the hour cometh, and now is, when the true worshippers shall worship the Father in spirit and in truth: for the Father seeketh such to worship him. God is a Spirit: and they that worship him must worship him in spirit and in truth.

The woman saith unto him, I know that Messias cometh, which is called Christ: when he is come, he will tell us all things.

Jesus saith unto her, I that speak unto thee am he.

And upon this came his disciples, and marvelled that he talked with the woman: yet no man said, What seekest thou? or, Why talkest thou with her?

The woman then left her waterpot, and went her way into the city, and saith to the men, Come, see a man, which told me all things that ever I did: is not this the Christ? Then they went out of the city, and came unto him.

In the mean while his disciples prayed him, saying, Master, eat.

But he said unto them, I have meat to eat that ye know not of.

Therefore said the disciples one to another, Hath any man brought him ought to eat?

Jesus saith unto them, My meat is to do the will of him that sent me, and to finish his work. Say not ye, There are yet four months, and then cometh harvest? behold, I say unto you, Lift up your eyes, and look on the fields; for they are white already to harvest. And he that reapeth receiveth wages, and gathereth fruit unto life eternal: that both he that soweth and he that reapeth may rejoice together. And herein is that saying true, One soweth, and another reapeth. I sent you to reap that whereon ye bestowed no labour: other men laboured, and ye are entered into their labours.

And many of the Samaritans of that city believed on him for the saying of the woman, which testified, He told me all that ever I did. So when the Samaritans were come unto him, they besought him that he would tarry with them: and he abode there two days. And many more believed because of his own word;

And said unto the woman, Now we believe, not because of thy saying: for we have heard him ourselves, and know that this is indeed the Christ, the Saviour of the world.
(John 4:1–42)

# This day is this Scripture fulfilled in your ears

And he came to Nazareth, where he had been brought up: and, as his custom was, he went into the synagogue on the sabbath day, and stood up for to read. And there was delivered unto him the book of the prophet Esaias. And when he had opened the book, he found the place where it was written,

The Spirit of the Lord is upon me,
because he hath anointed me
to preach the gospel to the poor;
he hath sent me to heal the brokenhearted,
to preach deliverance to the captives,
and recovering of sight to the blind,
to set at liberty them that are bruised,
To preach the acceptable year of the Lord.

And he closed the book, and he gave it again to the minister, and sat down. And the eyes of all them that were in the synagogue were fastened on him. And he began to say unto them, This day is this scripture fulfilled in your ears. And all bare him witness, and wondered at the gracious words which proceeded out of his mouth. And they said, Is not this Joseph's son?

And he said unto them, Ye will surely say unto me this proverb, Physician, heal thyself: whatsoever we have heard done in Capernaum, do also here in thy country. And he said, Verily I say unto you, No prophet is accepted in his own country. But I tell you of a truth, many widows were in Israel in the days of Elias, when the heaven was shut up three years and six months, when great famine was throughout all the land; But unto none of them was Elias sent, save unto Sarepta, a city of Sidon, unto a woman that was a widow. And many lepers were in Israel in the time of Eliseus the prophet; and none of them was cleansed, saving Naaman the Syrian.

And all they in the synagogue, when they heard these things, were filled with wrath, And rose up, and thrust him out of the city, and led him unto the brow of the hill whereon their city was built, that they might cast him down headlong. But he passing through the midst of them went his way, And came down to Capernaum, a city of Galilee, and taught them on the sabbath days.
(Luke 4:16–31)

*The Spirit of the Lord God is upon me; because the Lord hath anointed me to preach good tidings unto the meek; he hath sent me to bind up the brokenhearted, to proclaim liberty to the captives, and the opening of the prison to them that are bound; To proclaim the acceptable year of the Lord, and the day of vengeance of our God.*
*(Isaiah 61:1–2)*

# ollow Me

Now as he walked by the sea of Galilee, he saw Simon and Andrew his brother casting a net into the sea: for they were fishers. And Jesus said unto them, Come ye after me, and I will make you to become fishers of men. And straightway they forsook their nets, and followed him.

And when he had gone a little farther thence, he saw James the son of Zebedee, and John his brother, who also were in the ship mending their nets. And straightway he called them: and they left their father Zebedee in the ship with the hired servants, and went after him.
(Mark 1:16–20)

---

*If ye continue in my word, then are ye my disciples indeed;*
*And ye shall know the truth, and the truth shall make you free.*
*(John 8:31–32)*

# From henceforth thou shalt catch men

And it came to pass, that, as the people pressed upon him to hear the word of God, he stood by the lake of Gennesaret, And saw two ships standing by the lake: but the fishermen were gone out of them, and were washing their nets. And he entered into one of the ships, which was Simon's, and prayed him that he would thrust out a little from the land. And he sat down, and taught the people out of the ship.

Now when he had left speaking, he said unto Simon, Launch out into the deep, and let down your nets for a draught.

And Simon answering said unto him, Master, we have toiled all the night, and have taken nothing: nevertheless at thy word I will let down the net. And when they had this done, they inclosed a great multitude of fishes: and their net brake. And they beckoned unto their partners, which were in the other ship, that they should come and help them. And they came, and filled both the ships, so that they began to sink. When Simon Peter saw it, he fell down at Jesus' knees, saying, Depart from me; for I am a sinful man, O Lord.

For he was astonished, and all that were with him, at the draught of the fishes which they had taken: And so was also James, and John, the sons of Zebedee, which were partners with Simon. And Jesus said unto Simon, Fear not; from henceforth thou shalt catch men. And when they had brought their ships to land, they forsook all, and followed him. (Luke 5:1–11)

---

*But in a great house there are not only vessels of gold and of silver, but also of wood and of earth;*
*and some to honour, and some to dishonour. If a man therefore purge himself from these, he shall be*
*a vessel unto honour, sanctified, and meet for the master's use, and prepared unto every good work.*
*(2 Timothy 2:20–21)*

# Commandeth He even the unclean spirits

And they went into Capernaum; and straightway on the sabbath day he entered into the synagogue, and taught. And they were astonished at his doctrine: for he taught them as one that had authority, and not as the scribes.

And there was in their synagogue a man with an unclean spirit; and he cried out, Saying, Let us alone; what have we to do with thee, thou Jesus of Nazareth? art thou come to destroy us? I know thee who thou art, the Holy One of God.

And Jesus rebuked him, saying, Hold thy peace, and come out of him. And when the unclean spirit had torn him, and cried with a loud voice, he came out of him. And they were all amazed, insomuch that they questioned among themselves, saying, What thing is this? what new doctrine is this? for with authority commandeth he even the unclean spirits, and they do obey him. And immediately his fame spread abroad throughout all the region round about Galilee. (Mark 1:21–28)

---

*But if I with the finger of God cast out devils, no doubt the kingdom of God is come upon you.*
*(Luke 11:20)*

STRONG DELIV'RER, STRONG DELIV'RER, BE THOU STILL MY STRENGTH AND SHIELD

# And He laid His hands on every one of them, and healed them

Now when the sun was setting, all they that had any sick with divers diseases brought them unto him; and he laid his hands on every one of them, and healed them. And devils also came out of many, crying out, and saying, Thou art Christ the Son of God.

And he rebuking them suffered them not to speak: for they knew that he was Christ.

And when it was day, he departed and went into a desert place: and the people sought him, and came unto him, and stayed him, that he should not depart from them. And he said unto them, I must preach the kingdom of God to other cities also: for therefore am I sent. And he preached in the synagogues of Galilee.
(Luke 4:40–44)

---

*The blind receive their sight, and the lame walk, the lepers are cleansed, and the deaf hear, the dead are raised up, and the poor have the gospel preached to them. And blessed is he, whosoever shall not be offended in me.*
*(Matthew 11:5–6)*

That word, I say, ye know, which was published throughout all Judaea, and began from Galilee, after the baptism which John preached; How God anointed Jesus of Nazareth with the Holy Ghost and with power: who went about doing good, and healing all that were oppressed of the devil; for God was with him.

(Acts 10:37-38)

# I will; be thou clean

And it came to pass, when he was in a certain city, behold a man full of leprosy: who seeing Jesus fell on his face, and besought him, saying, Lord, if thou wilt, thou canst make me clean.

And he put forth his hand, and touched him, saying, I will: be thou clean. And immediately the leprosy departed from him. And he charged him to tell no man: but go, and shew thyself to the priest, and offer for thy cleansing, according as Moses commanded, for a testimony unto them.
(Luke 5:12–14)

---

*Bless the Lord, O my soul, and forget not all his benefits: Who forgiveth all thine iniquities; who healeth all thy diseases; Who redeemeth thy life from destruction; who crowneth thee with lovingkindness and tender mercies; Who satisfieth thy mouth with good things; so that thy youth is renewed like the eagle's.*
*(Psalm 103:2–5)*

# *He* withdrew himself into the wilderness, and prayed

*B*ut so much the more went there a fame abroad of him: and great multitudes came together to hear, and to be healed by him of their infirmities. And he withdrew himself into the wilderness, and prayed.
(Luke 5:15–16)

---

*O God, thou art my God; early will I seek thee: my soul thirsteth for thee, my flesh longeth for thee in a dry and thirsty land, where no water is; To see thy power and thy glory, so as I have seen thee in the sanctuary. Because thy lovingkindness is better than life, my lips shall praise thee. Thus will I bless thee while I live: I will lift up my hands in thy name.*
*(Psalm 63:1–4)*

# Thy sins are forgiven thee

And it came to pass on a certain day, as he was teaching, that there were Pharisees and doctors of the law sitting by, which were come out of every town of Galilee, and Judaea, and Jerusalem: and the power of the Lord was present to heal them. And, behold, men brought in a bed a man which was taken with a palsy: and they sought means to bring him in, and to lay him before him. And when they could not find by what way they might bring him in because of the multitude, they went upon the housetop, and let him down through the tiling with his couch into the midst before Jesus.

And when he saw their faith, he said unto him, Man, thy sins are forgiven thee.

And the scribes and the Pharisees began to reason, saying, Who is this which speaketh blasphemies? Who can forgive sins, but God alone?

But when Jesus perceived their thoughts, he answering said unto them, What reason ye in your hearts? Whether is easier, to say, Thy sins be forgiven thee; or to say, Rise up and walk? But that ye may know that the Son of man hath power upon earth to forgive sins, (he said unto the sick of the palsy,) I say unto thee, Arise, and take up thy couch, and go into thine house.

And immediately he rose up before them, and took up that whereon he lay, and departed to his own house, glorifying God. And they were all amazed, and they glorified God, and were filled with fear, saying, We have seen strange things to day.
(Luke 5:17–26)

---

*If thou, Lord, shouldest mark iniquities, O Lord, who shall stand?*
*But there is forgiveness with thee, that thou mayest be feared.*
*(Psalm 130:3–4)*

# Lord also of the Sabbath

And it came to pass, that he went through the corn fields on the sabbath day; and his disciples began, as they went, to pluck the ears of corn. And the Pharisees said unto him, Behold, why do they on the sabbath day that which is not lawful?

And he said unto them, Have ye never read what David did, when he had need, and was an hungred, he, and they that were with him? How he went into the house of God in the days of Abiathar the high priest, and did eat the shewbread, which is not lawful to eat but for the priests, and gave also to them which were with him?

And he said unto them, The sabbath was made for man, and not man for the sabbath: Therefore the Son of man is Lord also of the sabbath.
(Mark 2:23–28)

---

*Come unto me, all ye that labour and are heavy laden, and I will give you rest. Take my yoke upon you, and learn of me; for I am meek and lowly in heart: and ye shall find rest unto your souls. For my yoke is easy, and my burden is light.*
*(Matthew 11:28–30)*

# Rise, take up thy bed, and walk

After this there was a feast of the Jews; and Jesus went up to Jerusalem. Now there is at Jerusalem by the sheep market a pool, which is called in the Hebrew tongue Bethesda, having five porches. In these lay a great multitude of impotent folk, of blind, halt, withered, waiting for the moving of the water. For an angel went down at a certain season into the pool, and troubled the water: whosoever then first after the troubling of the water stepped in was made whole of whatsoever disease he had. And a certain man was there, which had an infirmity thirty and eight years. When Jesus saw him lie, and knew that he had been now a long time in that case, he saith unto him, Wilt thou be made whole?

The impotent man answered him, Sir, I have no man, when the water is troubled, to put me into the pool: but while I am coming, another steppeth down before me.

Jesus saith unto him, Rise, take up thy bed, and walk. And immediately the man was made whole, and took up his bed, and walked: and on the same day was the sabbath.

The Jews therefore said unto him that was cured, It is the sabbath day: it is not lawful for thee to carry thy bed.

He answered them, He that made me whole, the same said unto me, Take up thy bed, and walk.

Then asked they him, What man is that which said unto thee, Take up thy bed, and walk? And he that was healed wist not who it was: for Jesus had conveyed himself away, a multitude being in that place. Afterward Jesus findeth him in the temple, and said unto him, Behold, thou art made whole: sin no more, lest a worse thing come unto thee.

The man departed, and told the Jews that it was Jesus, which had made him whole.

And therefore did the Jews persecute Jesus, and sought to slay him, because he had done these things on the sabbath day.
(John 5:1–16)

---

*Fear thou not; for I am with thee: be not dismayed; for I am thy God: I will strengthen thee; yea, I will help thee; yea, I will uphold thee with the right hand of my righteousness.*
*(Isaiah 41:10)*

# To save life, or to kill?

And it came to pass also on another sabbath, that he entered into the synagogue and taught: and there was a man whose right hand was withered. And the scribes and Pharisees watched him, whether he would heal on the sabbath day; that they might find an accusation against him. But he knew their thoughts, and said to the man which had the withered hand, Rise up, and stand forth in the midst. And he arose and stood forth. Then said Jesus unto them, I will ask you one thing; Is it lawful on the sabbath days to do good, or to do evil? to save life, or to destroy it? And looking round about upon them all, he said unto the man, Stretch forth thy hand. And he did so: and his hand was restored whole as the other. And they were filled with madness; and communed one with another what they might do to Jesus. (Luke 6:6–11)

*For I am the Lord that healeth thee.*
*(Exodus 15:26)*

Heal me, O Lord, and I
shall be healed; save me,
and I shall be saved:
for thou art my praise.

(Jeremiah 17:14)

# Even as your Father which is in Heaven is perfect

And seeing the multitudes, he went up into a mountain: and when he was set, his disciples came unto him: And he opened his mouth, and taught them, saying,

Blessed are the poor in spirit: for theirs is the kingdom of heaven.

Blessed are they that mourn: for they shall be comforted.

Blessed are the meek: for they shall inherit the earth.

Blessed are they which do hunger and thirst after righteousness: for they shall be filled.

Blessed are the merciful: for they shall obtain mercy.

Blessed are the pure in heart: for they shall see God.

Blessed are the peacemakers: for they shall be called the children of God.

Blessed are they which are persecuted for righteousness' sake: for theirs is the kingdom of heaven.

Blessed are ye, when men shall revile you, and persecute you, and shall say all manner of evil against you falsely, for my sake. Rejoice, and be exceeding glad: for great is your reward in heaven: for so persecuted they the prophets which were before you.

Ye are the salt of the earth: but if the salt have lost his savour, wherewith shall it be salted? it is thenceforth good for nothing, but to be cast out, and to be trodden under foot of men.

Ye are the light of the world. A city that is set on an hill cannot be hid. Neither do men light a candle, and put it under a bushel, but on a candlestick; and it giveth light unto all that are in the house. Let your light so shine before men, that they may see your good works, and glorify your Father which is in heaven.

Think not that I am come to destroy the law, or the prophets: I am not come to destroy, but to fulfil. For verily I say unto you, Till heaven and earth pass, one jot or one tittle shall in no wise pass from the law, till all be fulfilled. Whosoever therefore shall break one of these least commandments, and shall teach men so, he shall be called the least in the kingdom of heaven: but whosoever shall do and teach them, the same shall be called great in the kingdom of heaven. For I say unto you, That except your righteousness shall exceed the righteousness of the scribes and Pharisees, ye shall in no case enter into the kingdom of heaven.

Ye have heard that it was said of them of old time, Thou shalt not kill; and whosoever shall kill shall be in danger of the judgment: But I say unto you, That whosoever is angry with his brother without a cause shall be in danger of the judgment: and whosoever shall say to his brother, Raca, shall be in danger of the council: but whosoever shall say, Thou fool, shall be in danger of hell fire. Therefore if thou bring thy gift to the altar, and there rememberest that thy brother hath ought against thee; Leave there thy gift before the altar, and go thy way; first be reconciled to thy brother, and then come and offer thy gift. Agree with thine adversary quickly, whiles thou art in the way with him; lest at any time the adversary deliver thee to the judge, and the judge deliver thee to the officer, and thou be cast into prison. Verily I say unto thee, Thou shalt by no means come out thence, till thou hast paid the uttermost farthing.

Ye have heard that it was said by them of old time, Thou shalt not commit adultery: But I say unto you, That whosoever looketh on a woman to lust after her hath committed adultery with her already in his heart. And if thy right eye offend thee, pluck it out, and cast it from thee: for it is profitable for thee that one of thy members should perish, and not that thy whole body should be cast into hell.

And if thy right hand offend thee, cut it off, and cast it from thee: for it is profitable for thee that one of thy members should perish, and not that thy whole body should be cast into hell.

It hath been said, Whosoever shall put away his wife, let him give her a writing of divorcement: But I say unto you, That whosoever shall put away his wife, saving for the cause of fornication, causeth her to commit adultery: and whosoever shall marry her that is divorced committeth adultery.

Again, ye have heard that it hath been said by them of old time, Thou shalt not forswear thyself, but shalt perform unto the Lord thine oaths: But I say unto you, Swear not at all; neither by heaven; for it is God's throne: Nor by the earth; for it is his footstool: neither by Jerusalem; for it is the city of the great King. Neither shalt thou swear by thy head, because thou canst not make one hair white or black. But let your communication be, Yea, yea; Nay, nay: for whatsoever is more than these cometh of evil.

Ye have heard that it hath been said, An eye for an eye, and a tooth for a tooth: But I say unto you, That ye resist not evil: but whosoever shall smite thee on thy right cheek, turn to him the other also. And if any man will sue thee at the law, and take away thy coat, let him have thy cloak also. And whosoever shall compel thee to go a mile, go with him twain. Give to him that asketh thee, and from him that would borrow of thee turn not thou away.

Ye have heard that it hath been said, Thou shalt love thy neighbour, and hate thine enemy. But I say unto you, Love your enemies, bless them that curse you, do good to them that hate you, and pray for them which despitefully use you, and persecute you; That ye may be the children of your Father which is in heaven: for he maketh his sun to rise on the evil and on the good, and sendeth rain on the just and on the unjust. For if ye love them which love you, what reward have ye? do not even the publicans the same? And if ye salute your brethren only, what do ye more than others? do not even the publicans so? Be ye therefore perfect, even as your Father which is in heaven is perfect.

(Matthew 5:1–48)

# As thou hast believed, so be it done unto thee

Now when he had ended all his sayings in the audience of the people, he entered into Capernaum. And a certain centurion's servant, who was dear unto him, was sick, and ready to die. And when he heard of Jesus, he sent unto him the elders of the Jews, beseeching him that he would come and heal his servant. And when they came to Jesus, they besought him instantly, saying, That he was worthy for whom he should do this: For he loveth our nation, and he hath built us a synagogue.

Then Jesus went with them. And when he was now not far from the house, the centurion sent friends to him, saying unto him, Lord, trouble not thyself: for I am not worthy that thou shouldest enter under my roof: Wherefore neither thought I myself worthy to come unto thee: but say in a word, and my servant shall be healed. For I also am a man set under authority, having under me soldiers, and I say unto one, Go, and he goeth; and to another, Come, and he cometh; and to my servant, Do this, and he doeth it.

When Jesus heard these things, he marvelled at him, and turned him about, and said unto the people that followed him, I say unto you, I have not found so great faith, no, not in Israel. And they that were sent, returning to the house, found the servant whole that had been sick.
(Luke 7:1–10)

---

*Now faith is the substance of things hoped for, the evidence of things not seen.*
*(Hebrews 11:1)*

# I say unto thee, Arise

And it came to pass the day after, that he went into a city called Nain; and many of his disciples went with him, and much people. Now when he came nigh to the gate of the city, behold, there was a dead man carried out, the only son of his mother, and she was a widow: and much people of the city was with her. And when the Lord saw her, he had compassion on her, and said unto her, Weep not. And he came and touched the bier: and they that bare him stood still. And he said, Young man, I say unto thee, Arise. And he that was dead sat up, and began to speak. And he delivered him to his mother.

And there came a fear on all: and they glorified God, saying, That a great prophet is risen up among us; and, That God hath visited his people.
(Luke 7:11–16)

---

*The thief cometh not, but for to steal, and to kill, and to destroy: I am come*
*that they might have life, and that they might have it more abundantly.*
*(John 10:10)*

# But to whom little is forgiven, the same loveth little

And one of the Pharisees desired him that he would eat with him. And he went into the Pharisee's house, and sat down to meat. And, behold, a woman in the city, which was a sinner, when she knew that Jesus sat at meat in the Pharisee's house, brought an alabaster box of ointment, And stood at his feet behind him weeping, and began to wash his feet with tears, and did wipe them with the hairs of her head, and kissed his feet, and anointed them with the ointment. Now when the Pharisee which had bidden him saw it, he spake within himself, saying, This man, if he were a prophet, would have known who and what manner of woman this is that toucheth him: for she is a sinner.

And Jesus answering said unto him, Simon, I have somewhat to say unto thee.

And he saith, Master, say on.

There was a certain creditor which had two debtors: the one owed five hundred pence, and the other fifty. And when they had nothing to pay, he frankly forgave them both. Tell me therefore, which of them will love him most?

Simon answered and said, I suppose that he, to whom he forgave most.

And he said unto him, Thou hast rightly judged. And he turned to the woman, and said unto Simon, Seest thou this woman? I entered into thine house, thou gavest me no water for my feet: but she hath washed my feet with tears, and wiped them with the hairs of her head. Thou gavest me no kiss: but this woman since the time I came in hath not ceased to kiss my feet. My head with oil thou didst not anoint: but this woman hath anointed my feet with ointment. Wherefore I say unto thee, Her sins, which are many, are forgiven; for she loved much: but to whom little is forgiven, the same loveth little.

And he said unto her, Thy sins are forgiven.

And they that sat at meat with him began to say within themselves, Who is this that forgiveth sins also?

And he said to the woman, Thy faith hath saved thee; go in peace. (Luke 7:36–50)

---

*Then Samuel took the horn of oil, and anointed him in the midst of his brethren:*
*and the Spirit of the Lord came upon David from that day forward.*
*(1 Samuel 16:13)*

# There went out a sower to sow

And he began again to teach by the sea side: and there was gathered unto him a great multitude, so that he entered into a ship, and sat in the sea; and the whole multitude was by the sea on the land. And he taught them many things by parables, and said unto them in his doctrine,

Hearken; Behold, there went out a sower to sow: And it came to pass, as he sowed, some fell by the way side, and the fowls of the air came and devoured it up. And some fell on stony ground, where it had not much earth; and immediately it sprang up, because it had no depth of earth: But when the sun was up, it was scorched; and because it had no root, it withered away. And some fell among thorns, and the thorns grew up, and choked it, and it yielded no fruit. And other fell on good ground, and did yield fruit that sprang up and increased; and brought forth, some thirty, and some sixty, and some an hundred.

And he said unto them, He that hath ears to hear, let him hear.

And when he was alone, they that were about him with the twelve asked of him the parable. And he said unto them, Unto you it is given to know the mystery of the kingdom of God: but unto them that are without, all these things are done in parables:

That seeing they may see, and not perceive; and hearing they may hear, and not understand; lest at any time they should be converted, and their sins should be forgiven them.

And he said unto them, Know ye not this parable? and how then will ye know all parables? The sower soweth the word. And these are they by the way side, where the word is sown; but when they have heard, Satan cometh immediately, and taketh away the word that was sown in their hearts. And these are they likewise which are sown on stony ground; who, when they have heard the word, immediately receive it with gladness; And have no root in themselves, and so endure but for a time: afterward, when affliction or persecution ariseth for the word's sake, immediately they are offended. And these are they which are sown among thorns; such as hear the word, And the cares of this world, and the deceitfulness of riches, and the lusts of other things entering in, choke the word, and it becometh unfruitful. And these are they which are sown on good ground; such as hear the word, and receive it, and bring forth fruit, some thirtyfold, some sixty, and some an hundred.

And he said unto them, Is a candle brought to be put under a bushel, or under a bed? and not to be set on a candlestick? For there is nothing hid, which shall not be manifested; neither was any thing kept secret, but that it should come abroad. If any man have ears to hear, let him hear.

And he said unto them, Take heed what ye hear: with what measure ye mete, it shall be measured to you: and unto you that hear shall more be given. For he that hath, to him shall be given: and he that hath not, from him shall be taken even that which he hath.

And he said, So is the kingdom of God, as if a man should cast seed into the ground; And should sleep, and rise night and day, and the seed should spring and grow up, he knoweth not how. For the earth bringeth forth fruit of herself; first the blade, then the ear, after that the full corn in the ear. But when the fruit is brought forth, immediately he putteth in the sickle, because the harvest is come. (Mark 4:1–29)

---

*And he said, Go, and tell this people, Hear ye indeed, but understand not; and see ye indeed, but perceive not. Make the heart of this people fat, and make their ears heavy, and shut their eyes; lest they see with their eyes, and hear with their ears, and understand with their heart, and convert, and be healed.*
*(Isaiah 6:9–10)*

# Peace, be still

And the same day, when the even was come, he saith unto them, Let us pass over unto the other side. And when they had sent away the multitude, they took him even as he was in the ship. And there were also with him other little ships. And there arose a great storm of wind, and the waves beat into the ship, so that it was now full. And he was in the hinder part of the ship, asleep on a pillow: and they awake him, and say unto him, Master, carest thou not that we perish?

And he arose, and rebuked the wind, and said unto the sea, Peace, be still. And the wind ceased, and there was a great calm. And he said unto them, Why are ye so fearful? how is it that ye have no faith? And they feared exceedingly, and said one to another, What manner of man is this, that even the wind and the sea obey him?
(Mark 4:35–41)

---

*Or who shut up the sea with doors, when it brake forth, as if it had issued out of the womb? When I made the cloud the garment thereof, and thick darkness a swaddlingband for it, And brake up for it my decreed place, and set bars and doors, And said, Hitherto shalt thou come, but no further: and here shall thy proud waves be stayed?*
*(Job 38:8–11)*

# Tell them how great things the Lord hath done for thee

And they came over unto the other side of the sea, into the country of the Gadarenes. And when he was come out of the ship, immediately there met him out of the tombs a man with an unclean spirit, Who had his dwelling among the tombs; and no man could bind him, no, not with chains: Because that he had been often bound with fetters and chains, and the chains had been plucked asunder by him, and the fetters broken in pieces: neither could any man tame him. And always, night and day, he was in the mountains, and in the tombs, crying, and cutting himself with stones.

But when he saw Jesus afar off, he ran and worshipped him, And cried with a loud voice, and said, What have I to do with thee, Jesus, thou Son of the most high God? I adjure thee by God, that thou torment me not.

For he said unto him, Come out of the man, thou unclean spirit. And he asked him, What is thy name?

And he answered, saying, My name is Legion: for we are many. And he besought him much that he would not send them away out of the country.

Now there was there nigh unto the mountains a great herd of swine feeding. And all the devils besought him, saying, Send us into the swine, that we may enter into them. And forthwith Jesus gave them leave. And the unclean spirits went out, and entered into the swine: and the herd ran violently down a steep place into the sea, (they were about two thousand;) and were choked in the sea.

And they that fed the swine fled, and told it in the city, and in the country. And they went out to see what it was that was done. And they come to Jesus, and see him that was possessed with the devil, and had the legion, sitting, and clothed, and in his right mind: and they were afraid. And they that saw it told them how it befell to him that was possessed with the devil, and also concerning the swine. And they began to pray him to depart out of their coasts.

And when he was come into the ship, he that had been possessed with the devil prayed him that he might be with him. Howbeit Jesus suffered him not, but saith unto him, Go home to thy friends, and tell them how great things the Lord hath done for thee, and hath had compassion on thee. And he departed, and began to publish in Decapolis how great things Jesus had done for him: and all men did marvel.

(Mark 5:1–20)

---

*But if I cast out devils by the Spirit of God, then the kingdom of God is come unto you. Or else how can one enter into a strong man's house, and spoil his goods, except he first bind the strong man? and then he will spoil his house.*
*(Matthew 12:28–29)*

# Thy faith hath made thee whole

And when Jesus was passed over again by ship unto the other side, much people gathered unto him: and he was nigh unto the sea. And, behold, there cometh one of the rulers of the synagogue, Jairus by name; and when he saw him, he fell at his feet, And besought him greatly, saying, My little daughter lieth at the point of death: I pray thee, come and lay thy hands on her, that she may be healed; and she shall live. And Jesus went with him; and much people followed him, and thronged him.

And a certain woman, which had an issue of blood twelve years, And had suffered many things of many physicians, and had spent all that she had, and was nothing bettered, but rather grew worse, When she had heard of Jesus, came in the press behind, and touched his garment. For she said, If I may touch but his clothes, I shall be whole.

And straightway the fountain of her blood was dried up; and she felt in her body that she was healed of that plague. And Jesus, immediately knowing in himself that virtue had gone out of him, turned him about in the press, and said, Who touched my clothes?

And his disciples said unto him, Thou seest the multitude thronging thee, and sayest thou, Who touched me?

And he looked round about to see her that had done this thing. But the woman fearing and trembling, knowing what was done in her, came and fell down before him, and told him all the truth. And he said unto her, Daughter, thy faith hath made thee whole; go in peace, and be whole of thy plague.
(Mark 5:21–34)

---

*The things which are impossible with men are possible with God.*
*(Luke 18:27)*

I sought the Lord, and he heard me, and
delivered me from all my fears. They looked
unto him, and were lightened: and their
faces were not ashamed. This poor man
cried, and the Lord heard him, and saved
him out of all his troubles.

(Psalm 34:4–6)

# Be not afraid; only believe

While he yet spake, there came from the ruler of the synagogue's house certain which said, Thy daughter is dead: why troublest thou the Master any further?

As soon as Jesus heard the word that was spoken, he saith unto the ruler of the synagogue, Be not afraid, only believe. And he suffered no man to follow him, save Peter, and James, and John the brother of James. And he cometh to the house of the ruler of the synagogue, and seeth the tumult, and them that wept and wailed greatly. And when he was come in, he saith unto them, Why make ye this ado, and weep? the damsel is not dead, but sleepeth.

And they laughed him to scorn. But when he had put them all out, he taketh the father and the mother of the damsel, and them that were with him, and entereth in where the damsel was lying. And he took the damsel by the hand, and said unto her, Talitha cumi; which is, being interpreted, Damsel, I say unto thee, arise. And straightway the damsel arose, and walked; for she was of the age of twelve years. And they were astonished with a great astonishment. And he charged them straitly that no man should know it; and commanded that something should be given her to eat.
(Mark 5:35–43)

---

*God, who quickeneth the dead, and calleth those things which be not as though they were.*
*(Romans 4:17)*

# Into a desert place apart

At that time Herod the tetrarch heard of the fame of Jesus, And said unto his servants, This is John the Baptist; he is risen from the dead; and therefore mighty works do shew forth themselves in him. For Herod had laid hold on John, and bound him, and put him in prison for Herodias' sake, his brother Philip's wife. For John said unto him, It is not lawful for thee to have her. And when he would have put him to death, he feared the multitude, because they counted him as a prophet.

But when Herod's birthday was kept, the daughter of Herodias danced before them, and pleased Herod. Whereupon he promised with an oath to give her whatsoever she would ask.

And she, being before instructed of her mother, said, Give me here John Baptist's head in a charger.

And the king was sorry: nevertheless for the oath's sake, and them which sat with him at meat, he commanded it to be given her. And he sent, and beheaded John in the prison. And his head was brought in a charger, and given to the damsel: and she brought it to her mother. And his disciples came, and took up the body, and buried it, and went and told Jesus.

When Jesus heard of it, he departed thence by ship into a desert place apart.
(Matthew 14:1–13)

---

*For this is he, of whom it is written, Behold, I send my messenger before thy*
*face, which shall prepare thy way before thee. Verily I say unto you, Among them*
*that are born of women there hath not risen a greater than John the Baptist:*
*notwithstanding he that is least in the kingdom of heaven is greater than he.*
*(Matthew 11:10–11)*

# They need not depart; give ye them to eat

And when the people had heard thereof, they followed him on foot out of the cities. And Jesus went forth, and saw a great multitude, and was moved with compassion toward them, and he healed their sick. And when it was evening, his disciples came to him, saying, This is a desert place, and the time is now past; send the multitude away, that they may go into the villages, and buy themselves victuals.

But Jesus said unto them, They need not depart; give ye them to eat.

And they say unto him, We have here but five loaves, and two fishes.

He said, Bring them hither to me. And he commanded the multitude to sit down on the grass, and took the five loaves, and the two fishes, and looking up to heaven, he blessed, and brake, and gave the loaves to his disciples, and the disciples to the multitude. And they did all eat, and were filled: and they took up of the fragments that remained twelve baskets full. And they that had eaten were about five thousand men, beside women and children. (Matthew 14:13–21)

---

*The Lord is my shepherd; I shall not want. He maketh me to lie down in green pastures: he leadeth me beside the still waters. He restoreth my soul: he leadeth me in the paths of righteousness for his name's sake. (Psalm 23:1–3)*

*But my God shall supply all your need according to his riches in glory by Christ Jesus. (Philippians 4:19)*

# Be of good cheer; It is I

And straightway Jesus constrained his disciples to get into a ship, and to go before him unto the other side, while he sent the multitudes away. And when he had sent the multitudes away, he went up into a mountain apart to pray: and when the evening was come, he was there alone. But the ship was now in the midst of the sea, tossed with waves: for the wind was contrary.

And in the fourth watch of the night Jesus went unto them, walking on the sea. And when the disciples saw him walking on the sea, they were troubled, saying, It is a spirit; and they cried out for fear.

But straightway Jesus spake unto them, saying, Be of good cheer; it is I; be not afraid. (Matthew 14:22–27)

---

*For God hath not given us the spirit of fear; but of power, and of love, and of a sound mind.*
*(2 Timothy 1:7)*

The floods have lifted up, O Lord, the
floods have lifted up their voice; the floods
lift up their waves. The Lord on high is
mightier than the noise of many waters, yea
than the mighty waves of the sea.

(Psalm 93:3-4)

# O thou of little faith, wherefore didst thou doubt?

And Peter answered him and said, Lord, if it be thou, bid me come unto thee on the water.

And he said, Come. And when Peter was come down out of the ship, he walked on the water, to go to Jesus. But when he saw the wind boisterous, he was afraid; and beginning to sink, he cried, saying, Lord, save me.

And immediately Jesus stretched forth his hand, and caught him, and said unto him, O thou of little faith, wherefore didst thou doubt? And when they were come into the ship, the wind ceased. Then they that were in the ship came and worshipped him, saying, Of a truth thou art the Son of God.
(Matthew 14:28–33)

Then they willingly received him into the ship: and immediately the ship was at the land whither they went.
(John 6:21)

*The eyes of the Lord are upon the righteous, and his ears are open unto their cry.*
*(Psalm 34:15)*

WHEN THE STRONG TIDES LIFT, AND THE CABLES STRAIN, WILL YOUR ANCHOR DRIFT, OR FIRM REMAIN?

There is no king saved by the multitude of an host: a mighty man is not delivered by much strength. An horse is a vain thing for safety: neither shall he deliver any by his great strength. Behold, the eye of the Lord is upon them that fear him, upon them that hope in his mercy; To deliver their soul from death, and to keep them alive in famine. Our soul waiteth for the Lord: he is our help and our shield. For our heart shall rejoice in him, because we have trusted in his holy name. Let thy mercy, O Lord, be upon us, according as we hope in thee.

(Psalm 33:16-22)

# I am the bread of life

The day following, when the people which stood on the other side of the sea saw that there was none other boat there, save that one whereinto his disciples were entered, and that Jesus went not with his disciples into the boat, but that his disciples were gone away alone; (Howbeit there came other boats from Tiberias nigh unto the place where they did eat bread, after that the Lord had given thanks:) When the people therefore saw that Jesus was not there, neither his disciples, they also took shipping, and came to Capernaum, seeking for Jesus. And when they had found him on the other side of the sea, they said unto him, Rabbi, when camest thou hither?

Jesus answered them and said, Verily, verily, I say unto you, Ye seek me, not because ye saw the miracles, but because ye did eat of the loaves, and were filled. Labour not for the meat which perisheth, but for that meat which endureth unto everlasting life, which the Son of man shall give unto you: for him hath God the Father sealed.

Then said they unto him, What shall we do, that we might work the works of God?

Jesus answered and said unto them, This is the work of God, that ye believe on him whom he hath sent.

They said therefore unto him, What sign shewest thou then, that we may see, and believe thee? what dost thou work? Our fathers did eat manna in the desert; as it is written, He gave them bread from heaven to eat.

Then Jesus said unto them, Verily, verily, I say unto you, Moses gave you not that bread from heaven; but my Father giveth you the true bread from heaven. For the bread of God is he which cometh down from heaven, and giveth life unto the world.

Then said they unto him, Lord, evermore give us this bread.

And Jesus said unto them, I am the bread of life: he that cometh to me shall never hunger; and he that believeth on me shall never thirst. But I said unto you, That ye also have seen me, and believe not. All that the Father giveth me shall come to me; and him that cometh to me I will in no wise cast out. For I came down from heaven, not to do mine own will, but the will of him that sent me. And this is the Father's will which hath sent me, that of all which he hath given me I should lose nothing, but should raise it up again at the last day. And this is the will of him that sent me, that every one which seeth the Son, and believeth on him, may have everlasting life: and I will raise him up at the last day.

The Jews then murmured at him, because he said, I am the bread which came down from heaven. And they said, Is not this Jesus, the son of Joseph, whose father and mother we know? how is it then that he saith, I came down from heaven?

Jesus therefore answered and said unto them, Murmur not among yourselves. No man can come to me, except the Father which hath sent me draw him: and I will raise him up at the last day. It is written in the prophets, And they shall be all taught of God. Every man therefore that hath heard, and hath learned of the Father, cometh unto me. Not that any man hath seen the Father, save he which is of God, he hath seen the Father. Verily, verily, I say unto you, He that believeth on me hath everlasting life. I am that bread of life. Your fathers did eat manna in the wilderness, and are dead. This is the bread which cometh down from heaven, that a man may eat thereof, and not die. I am the living bread which came down from heaven: if any man eat of this bread, he shall live for ever: and the bread that I will give is my flesh, which I will give for the life of the world.

The Jews therefore strove among themselves, saying, How can this man give us his flesh to eat?

Then Jesus said unto them, Verily, verily, I say unto you, Except ye eat the flesh of the Son of man, and drink his blood, ye have no life in you. Whoso eateth my flesh, and drinketh my blood, hath eternal life; and I will raise him up at the last day.

For my flesh is meat indeed, and my blood is drink indeed. He that eateth my flesh, and drinketh my blood, dwelleth in me, and I in him. As the living Father hath sent me, and I live by the Father: so he that eateth me, even he shall live by me.

This is that bread which came down from heaven: not as your fathers did eat manna, and are dead: he that eateth of this bread shall live for ever.

These things said he in the synagogue, as he taught in Capernaum.

Many therefore of his disciples, when they had heard this, said, This is an hard saying; who can hear it?

When Jesus knew in himself that his disciples murmured at it, he said unto them, Doth this offend you? What and if ye shall see the Son of man ascend up where he was before? It is the spirit that quickeneth; the flesh profiteth nothing: the words that I speak unto you, they are spirit, and they are life. But there are some of you that believe not. For Jesus knew from the beginning who they were that believed not, and who should betray him. And he said, Therefore said I unto you, that no man can come unto me, except it were given unto him of my Father.

From that time many of his disciples went back, and walked no more with him.

Then said Jesus unto the twelve, Will ye also go away?

Then Simon Peter answered him, Lord, to whom shall we go? thou hast the words of eternal life. And we believe and are sure that thou art that Christ, the Son of the living God.

Jesus answered them, Have not I chosen you twelve, and one of you is a devil? He spake of Judas Iscariot the son of Simon: for he it was that should betray him, being one of the twelve.
(John 6:22–71)

# Owoman, great is thy faith

Then Jesus went thence, and departed into the coasts of Tyre and Sidon. And, behold, a woman of Canaan came out of the same coasts, and cried unto him, saying, Have mercy on me, O Lord, thou son of David; my daughter is grievously vexed with a devil.

But he answered her not a word.

And his disciples came and besought him, saying, Send her away; for she crieth after us.

But he answered and said, I am not sent but unto the lost sheep of the house of Israel.

Then came she and worshipped him, saying, Lord, help me.

But he answered and said, It is not meet to take the children's bread, and to cast it to dogs.

And she said, Truth, Lord: yet the dogs eat of the crumbs which fall from their masters' table.

Then Jesus answered and said unto her, O woman, great is thy faith: be it unto thee even as thou wilt. And her daughter was made whole from that very hour.
(Matthew 15:21–28)

---

*But without faith it is impossible to please him: for he that cometh to God must believe that he is, and that he is a rewarder of them that diligently seek him.*
*(Hebrews 11:6)*

# *He* maketh both the deaf to hear, and the dumb to speak

And again, departing from the coasts of Tyre and Sidon, he came unto the sea of Galilee, through the midst of the coasts of Decapolis. And they bring unto him one that was deaf, and had an impediment in his speech; and they beseech him to put his hand upon him. And he took him aside from the multitude, and put his fingers into his ears, and he spit, and touched his tongue; And looking up to heaven, he sighed, and saith unto him, Ephphatha, that is, Be opened.

And straightway his ears were opened, and the string of his tongue was loosed, and he spake plain. And he charged them that they should tell no man: but the more he charged them, so much the more a great deal they published it; And were beyond measure astonished, saying, He hath done all things well: he maketh both the deaf to hear, and the dumb to speak.
(Mark 7:31–37)

---

*Then the eyes of the blind shall be opened, and the ears of the deaf shall be unstopped. Then shall the lame man leap as an hart, and the tongue of the dumb sing: for in the wilderness shall waters break out, and streams in the desert.*
*(Isaiah 35:5–6)*

# And they did all eat, and were filled

And Jesus departed from thence, and came nigh unto the sea of Galilee; and went up into a mountain, and sat down there. And great multitudes came unto him, having with them those that were lame, blind, dumb, maimed, and many others, and cast them down at Jesus' feet; and he healed them: Insomuch that the multitude wondered, when they saw the dumb to speak, the maimed to be whole, the lame to walk, and the blind to see: and they glorified the God of Israel.

Then Jesus called his disciples unto him, and said, I have compassion on the multitude, because they continue with me now three days, and have nothing to eat: and I will not send them away fasting, lest they faint in the way.

And his disciples say unto him, Whence should we have so much bread in the wilderness, as to fill so great a multitude?

And Jesus saith unto them, How many loaves have ye?

And they said, Seven, and a few little fishes.

And he commanded the multitude to sit down on the ground. And he took the seven loaves and the fishes, and gave thanks, and brake them, and gave to his disciples, and the disciples to the multitude. And they did all eat, and were filled: and they took up of the broken meat that was left seven baskets full. And they that did eat were four thousand men, beside women and children. And he sent away the multitude, and took ship, and came into the coasts of Magdala. (Matthew 15:29–39)

---

*Now unto him that is able to do exceeding abundantly above all that we ask*
*or think, according to the power that worketh in us, Unto him be glory in the*
*church by Christ Jesus throughout all ages, world without end. Amen.*
*(Ephesians 3:20–21)*

# Hear ye Him

When Jesus came into the coasts of Caesarea Philippi, he asked his disciples, saying, Whom do men say that I the Son of man am?

And they said, Some say that thou art John the Baptist: some, Elias; and others, Jeremias, or one of the prophets.

He saith unto them, But whom say ye that I am?

And Simon Peter answered and said, Thou art the Christ, the Son of the living God.

And Jesus answered and said unto him, Blessed art thou, Simon Barjona: for flesh and blood hath not revealed it unto thee, but my Father which is in heaven. And I say also unto thee, That thou art Peter, and upon this rock I will build my church; and the gates of hell shall not prevail against it. And I will give unto thee the keys of the kingdom of heaven: and whatsoever thou shalt bind on earth shall be bound in heaven: and whatsoever thou shalt loose on earth shall be loosed in heaven.

Then charged he his disciples that they should tell no man that he was Jesus the Christ.

From that time forth began Jesus to shew unto his disciples, how that he must go unto Jerusalem, and suffer many things of the elders and chief priests and scribes, and be killed, and be raised again the third day.

Then Peter took him, and began to rebuke him, saying, Be it far from thee, Lord: this shall not be unto thee.

But he turned, and said unto Peter, Get thee behind me, Satan: thou art an offence unto me: for thou savourest not the things that be of God, but those that be of men.

Then said Jesus unto his disciples, If any man will come after me, let him deny himself, and take up his cross, and follow me. For whosoever will save his life shall lose it: and whosoever will lose his life for my sake shall find it. For what is a man profited, if he shall gain the whole world, and lose his own soul? or what shall a man give in exchange for his soul? For the Son of man shall come in the glory of his Father with his angels; and then he shall reward every man according to his works. Verily I say unto you, There be some standing here, which shall not taste of death, till they see the Son of man coming in his kingdom.

And after six days Jesus taketh Peter, James, and John his brother, and bringeth them up into an high mountain apart, And was transfigured before them: and his face did shine as the sun, and his raiment was white as the light. And, behold, there appeared unto them Moses and Elias talking with him. Then answered Peter, and said unto Jesus, Lord, it is good for us to be here: if thou wilt, let us make here three tabernacles; one for thee, and one for Moses, and one for Elias.

While he yet spake, behold, a bright cloud overshadowed them: and behold a voice out of the cloud, which said, This is my beloved Son, in whom I am well pleased; hear ye him. And when the disciples heard it, they fell on their face, and were sore afraid. And Jesus came and touched them, and said, Arise, and be not afraid. And when they had lifted up their eyes, they saw no man, save Jesus only.

And as they came down from the mountain, Jesus charged them, saying, Tell the vision to no man, until the Son of man be risen again from the dead.

And his disciples asked him, saying, Why then say the scribes that Elias must first come?

And Jesus answered and said unto them, Elias truly shall first come, and restore all things. But I say unto you, That Elias is come already, and they knew him not, but have done unto him whatsoever they listed. Likewise shall also the Son of man suffer of them. Then the disciples understood that he spake unto them of John the Baptist.
(Matthew 16:13–Matthew 17:13)

---

*God, who at sundry times and in divers manners spake in time past unto the fathers by the prophets, Hath in these last days spoken unto us by his Son, whom he hath appointed heir of all things, by whom also he made the worlds; Who being the brightness of his glory, and the express image of his person, and upholding all things by the word of his power, when he had by himself purged our sins, sat down on the right hand of the Majesty on high: Being made so much better than the angels, as he hath by inheritance obtained a more excellent name than they.*
*(Hebrews 1:1–4)*

Ye men of Israel, hear these words; Jesus of Nazareth, a man approved of God among you by miracles and wonders and signs, which God did by him in the midst of you, as ye yourselves also know: Him, being delivered by the determinate counsel and foreknowledge of God, ye have taken, and by wicked hands have crucified and slain: Whom God hath raised up, having loosed the pains of death: because it was not possible that he should be holden of it.

(Acts 2:22-24)

For he received from God the Father honour and glory, when there came such a voice to him from the excellent glory, This is my beloved Son in whom I am well pleased. And this voice which came from heaven we heard, when we were with him in the holy mount. We have also a more sure word of prophecy; whereunto ye do well that ye take heed, as unto a light that shineth in a dark place, until the day dawn, and the day star arise in your hearts: Knowing this first, that no prophecy of the scripture is of any private interpretation. For the prophecy came not in old time by the will of man: but holy men of God spake as they were moved by the Holy Ghost.

(2 Peter 1:17-21)

# All things are possible to him that believeth

And when he came to his disciples, he saw a great multitude about them, and the scribes questioning with them. And straightway all the people, when they beheld him, were greatly amazed, and running to him saluted him. And he asked the scribes, What question ye with them?

And one of the multitude answered and said, Master, I have brought unto thee my son, which hath a dumb spirit; And wheresoever he taketh him, he teareth him: and he foameth, and gnasheth with his teeth, and pineth away: and I spake to thy disciples that they should cast him out; and they could not.

He answereth him, and saith, O faithless generation, how long shall I be with you? how long shall I suffer you? bring him unto me. And they brought him unto him: and when he saw him, straightway the spirit tare him; and he fell on the ground, and wallowed foaming.

And he asked his father, How long is it ago since this came unto him?

And he said, Of a child. And ofttimes it hath cast him into the fire, and into the waters, to destroy him: but if thou canst do any thing, have compassion on us, and help us.

Jesus said unto him, If thou canst believe, all things are possible to him that believeth.

And straightway the father of the child cried out, and said with tears, Lord, I believe; help thou mine unbelief.

When Jesus saw that the people came running together, he rebuked the foul spirit, saying unto him, Thou dumb and deaf spirit, I charge thee, come out of him, and enter no more into him. And the spirit cried, and rent him sore, and came out of him: and he was as one dead; insomuch that many said, He is dead. But Jesus took him by the hand, and lifted him up; and he arose.

And when he was come into the house, his disciples asked him privately, Why could not we cast him out?

And he said unto them, This kind can come forth by nothing, but by prayer and fasting.
(Mark 9:14–29)

---

*I am crucified with Christ: nevertheless I live; yet not I, but Christ liveth in me: and the life which*
*I now live in the flesh I live by the faith of the Son of God, who loved me, and gave himself for me.*
*(Galatians 2:20)*

# Neither do I condemn thee, go, and sin no more

And early in the morning he came again into the temple, and all the people came unto him; and he sat down, and taught them. And the scribes and Pharisees brought unto him a woman taken in adultery; and when they had set her in the midst, They say unto him, Master, this woman was taken in adultery, in the very act. Now Moses in the law commanded us, that such should be stoned: but what sayest thou? This they said, tempting him, that they might have to accuse him. But Jesus stooped down, and with his finger wrote on the ground, as though he heard them not.

So when they continued asking him, he lifted up himself, and said unto them, He that is without sin among you, let him first cast a stone at her. And again he stooped down, and wrote on the ground. And they which heard it, being convicted by their own conscience, went out one by one, beginning at the eldest, even unto the last: and Jesus was left alone, and the woman standing in the midst. When Jesus had lifted up himself, and saw none but the woman, he said unto her, Woman, where are those thine accusers? hath no man condemned thee?

She said, No man, Lord.

And Jesus said unto her, Neither do I condemn thee: go, and sin no more.

Then spake Jesus again unto them, saying, I am the light of the world: he that followeth me shall not walk in darkness, but shall have the light of life.

The Pharisees therefore said unto him, Thou bearest record of thyself; thy record is not true.

Jesus answered and said unto them, Though I bear record of myself, yet my record is true: for I know whence I came, and whither I go; but ye cannot tell whence I come, and whither I go. Ye judge after the flesh; I judge no man. And yet if I judge, my judgment is true: for I am not alone, but I and the Father that sent me. It is also written in your law, that the testimony of two men is true. I am one that bear witness of myself, and the Father that sent me beareth witness of me.

Then said they unto him, Where is thy Father?

Jesus answered, Ye neither know me, nor my Father: if ye had known me, ye should have known my Father also.

These words spake Jesus in the treasury, as he taught in the temple: and no man laid hands on him; for his hour was not yet come. (John 8:2–20)

---

*For when ye were the servants of sin, ye were free from righteousness. What fruit had ye then in those things whereof ye are now ashamed? for the end of those things is death. But now being made free from sin, and become servants to God, ye have your fruit unto holiness, and the end everlasting life. For the wages of sin is death; but the gift of God is eternal life through Jesus Christ our Lord. (Romans 6:20–23)*

# Were there not ten cleansed?

And it came to pass, as he went to Jerusalem, that he passed through the midst of Samaria and Galilee. And as he entered into a certain village, there met him ten men that were lepers, which stood afar off: And they lifted up their voices, and said, Jesus, Master, have mercy on us.

And when he saw them, he said unto them, Go shew yourselves unto the priests. And it came to pass, that, as they went, they were cleansed.

And one of them, when he saw that he was healed, turned back, and with a loud voice glorified God, And fell down on his face at his feet, giving him thanks: and he was a Samaritan.

And Jesus answering said, Were there not ten cleansed? but where are the nine? There are not found that returned to give glory to God, save this stranger. And he said unto him, Arise, go thy way: thy faith hath made thee whole.
(Luke 17:11–19)

*The Lord is gracious, and full of compassion; slow to anger, and of great*
*mercy. The Lord is good to all: and his tender mercies are over all his works.*
*All thy works shall praise thee, O Lord; and thy saints shall bless thee.*
*(Psalm 145:8–10)*

# One thing is needful

Now it came to pass, as they went, that he entered into a certain village: and a certain woman named Martha received him into her house. And she had a sister called Mary, which also sat at Jesus' feet, and heard his word. But Martha was cumbered about much serving, and came to him, and said, Lord, dost thou not care that my sister hath left me to serve alone? bid her therefore that she help me.

  And Jesus answered and said unto her, Martha, Martha, thou art careful and troubled about many things: But one thing is needful: and Mary hath chosen that good part, which shall not be taken away from her.
(Luke 10:38–42)

*All scripture is given by inspiration of God, and is profitable for doctrine,*
*for reproof, for correction, for instruction in righteousness: That the man*
*of God may be perfect, thoroughly furnished unto all good works.*
*(2 Timothy 3:16–17)*

# Our Father which art in heaven

And it came to pass, that, as he was praying in a certain place, when he ceased, one of his disciples said unto him, Lord, teach us to pray, as John also taught his disciples.

And he said unto them, When ye pray, say,
Our Father which art in heaven,
Hallowed be thy name.
Thy kingdom come.
Thy will be done,
as in heaven, so in earth.
Give us day by day our daily bread.
And forgive us our sins;
for we also forgive every one that is indebted to us.
And lead us not into temptation;
but deliver us from evil.

And he said unto them, Which of you shall have a friend, and shall go unto him at midnight, and say unto him, Friend, lend me three loaves;

For a friend of mine in his journey is come to me, and I have nothing to set before him? And he from within shall answer and say, Trouble me not: the door is now shut, and my children are with me in bed; I cannot rise and give thee. I say unto you, Though he will not rise and give him, because he is his friend, yet because of his importunity he will rise and give him as many as he needeth.

And I say unto you, Ask, and it shall be given you; seek, and ye shall find; knock, and it shall be opened unto you. For every one that asketh receiveth; and he that seeketh findeth; and to him that knocketh it shall be opened. If a son shall ask bread of any of you that is a father, will he give him a stone? or if he ask a fish, will he for a fish give him a serpent? Or if he shall ask an egg, will he offer him a scorpion? If ye then, being evil, know how to give good gifts unto your children: how much more shall your heavenly Father give the Holy Spirit to them that ask him? (Luke 11:1–13)

*for your Father knoweth what things ye have need of, before ye ask him.*
*(Matthew 6:8)*

# I am the light of the world

And as Jesus passed by, he saw a man which was blind from his birth. And his disciples asked him, saying, Master, who did sin, this man, or his parents, that he was born blind?

Jesus answered, Neither hath this man sinned, nor his parents: but that the works of God should be made manifest in him. I must work the works of him that sent me, while it is day: the night cometh, when no man can work. As long as I am in the world, I am the light of the world.

When he had thus spoken, he spat on the ground, and made clay of the spittle, and he anointed the eyes of the blind man with the clay, And said unto him, Go, wash in the pool of Siloam, (which is by interpretation, Sent.) He went his way therefore, and washed, and came seeing.

The neighbours therefore, and they which before had seen him that he was blind, said, Is not this he that sat and begged?

Some said, This is he: others said, He is like him: but he said, I am he.

Therefore said they unto him, How were thine eyes opened?

He answered and said, A man that is called Jesus made clay, and anointed mine eyes, and said unto me, Go to the pool of Siloam, and wash: and I went and washed, and I received sight.

Then said they unto him, Where is he?

He said, I know not.

They brought to the Pharisees him that aforetime was blind. And it was the sabbath day when Jesus made the clay, and opened his eyes. Then again the Pharisees also asked him how he had received his sight. He said unto them, He put clay upon mine eyes, and I washed, and do see.

Therefore said some of the Pharisees, This man is not of God, because he keepeth not the sabbath day.

Others said, How can a man that is a sinner do such miracles? And there was a division among them.

They say unto the blind man again, What sayest thou of him, that he hath opened thine eyes?

He said, He is a prophet.

But the Jews did not believe concerning him, that he had been blind, and received his sight, until they called the parents of him that had received his sight. And they asked them, saying, Is this your son, who ye say was born blind? how then doth he now see?

His parents answered them and said, We know that this is our son, and that he was born blind: But by what means he now seeth, we know not; or who hath opened his eyes, we know not: he is of age; ask him: he shall speak for himself. These words spake his parents, because they feared the Jews: for the Jews had agreed already, that if any man did confess that he was Christ, he should be put out of the synagogue. Therefore said his parents, He is of age; ask him.

Then again called they the man that was blind, and said unto him, Give God the praise: we know that this man is a sinner.

He answered and said, Whether he be a sinner or no, I know not: one thing I know, that, whereas I was blind, now I see.

Then said they to him again, What did he to thee? how opened he thine eyes?

He answered them, I have told you already, and ye did not hear: wherefore would ye hear it again? will ye also be his disciples?

Then they reviled him, and said, Thou art his disciple; but we are Moses' disciples. We know that God spake unto Moses: as for this fellow, we know not from whence he is.

The man answered and said unto them, Why herein is a marvellous thing, that ye know not from whence he is, and yet he hath opened mine eyes. Now we know that God heareth not sinners: but if any man be a worshipper of God, and doeth his will, him he heareth. Since the world began was it not heard that any man opened the eyes of one that was born blind. If this man were not of God, he could do nothing.

They answered and said unto him, Thou wast altogether born in sins, and dost thou teach us? And they cast him out.

Jesus heard that they had cast him out; and when he had found him, he said unto him, Dost thou believe on the Son of God?

He answered and said, Who is he, Lord, that I might believe on him?

And Jesus said unto him, Thou hast both seen him, and it is he that talketh with thee. And he said, Lord, I believe. And he worshipped him.

And Jesus said, For judgment I am come into this world, that they which see not might see; and that they which see might be made blind.

And some of the Pharisees which were with him heard these words, and said unto him, Are we blind also?

Jesus said unto them, If ye were blind, ye should have no sin: but now ye say, We see; therefore your sin remaineth.
(John 9:1–41)

# I am the door

Verily, verily, I say unto you, He that entereth not by the door into the sheepfold, but climbeth up some other way, the same is a thief and a robber. But he that entereth in by the door is the shepherd of the sheep. To him the porter openeth; and the sheep hear his voice: and he calleth his own sheep by name, and leadeth them out. And when he putteth forth his own sheep, he goeth before them, and the sheep follow him: for they know his voice. And a stranger will they not follow, but will flee from him: for they know not the voice of strangers. This parable spake Jesus unto them: but they understood not what things they were which he spake unto them.

Then said Jesus unto them again, Verily, verily, I say unto you, I am the door of the sheep. All that ever came before me are thieves and robbers: but the sheep did not hear them. I am the door: by me if any man enter in, he shall be saved, and shall go in and out, and find pasture. The thief cometh not, but for to steal, and to kill, and to destroy: I am come that they might have life, and that they might have it more abundantly.

I am the good shepherd: the good shepherd giveth his life for the sheep. But he that is an hireling, and not the shepherd, whose own the sheep are not, seeth the wolf coming, and leaveth the sheep, and fleeth: and the wolf catcheth them, and scattereth the sheep. The hireling fleeth, because he is an hireling, and careth not for the sheep. I am the good shepherd, and know my sheep, and am known of mine. As the Father knoweth me, even so know I the Father: and I lay down my life for the sheep. And other sheep I have, which are not of this fold: them also I must bring, and they shall hear my voice; and there shall be one fold, and one shepherd.

Therefore doth my Father love me, because I lay down my life, that I might take it again. No man taketh it from me, but I lay it down of myself. I have power to lay it down, and I have power to take it again. This commandment have I received of my Father.

There was a division therefore again among the Jews for these sayings. And many of them said, He hath a devil, and is mad; why hear ye him?

Others said, These are not the words of him that hath a devil. Can a devil open the eyes of the blind?

And it was at Jerusalem the feast of the dedication, and it was winter. And Jesus walked in the temple in Solomon's porch. Then came the Jews round about him, and said unto him, How long dost thou make us to doubt? If thou be the Christ, tell us plainly.

Jesus answered them, I told you, and ye believed not: the works that I do in my Father's name, they bear witness of me. But ye believe not, because ye are not of my sheep, as I said unto you. My sheep hear my voice, and I know them, and they follow me: And I give unto them eternal life; and they shall never perish, neither shall any man pluck them out of my hand. My Father, which gave them me, is greater than all; and no man is able to pluck them out of my Father's hand. I and my Father are one.

Then the Jews took up stones again to stone him. Jesus answered them, Many good works have I shewed you from my Father; for which of those works do ye stone me?

The Jews answered him, saying, For a good work we stone thee not; but for blasphemy; and because that thou, being a man, makest thyself God.

Jesus answered them, Is it not written in your law, I said, Ye are gods? If he called them gods, unto whom the word of God came, and the scripture cannot be broken; Say ye of him, whom the Father hath sanctified, and sent into the world, Thou blasphemest; because I said, I am the Son of God? If I do not the works of my Father, believe me not. But if I do, though ye believe not me, believe the works: that ye may know, and believe, that the Father is in me, and I in him. Therefore they sought again to take him: but he escaped out of their hand,

And went away again beyond Jordan into the place where John at first baptized; and there he abode. And many resorted unto him, and said, John did no miracle: but all things that John spake of this man were true. And many believed on him there.
(John 10:1–42)

*I am the way, the truth, and the life: no man cometh unto the Father, but by me.*
*(John 14:6)*

# I am the resurrection, and the life

Now a certain man was sick, named Lazarus, of Bethany, the town of Mary and her sister Martha. (It was that Mary which anointed the Lord with ointment, and wiped his feet with her hair, whose brother Lazarus was sick.) Therefore his sisters sent unto him, saying, Lord, behold, he whom thou lovest is sick.

When Jesus heard that, he said, This sickness is not unto death, but for the glory of God, that the Son of God might be glorified thereby.

Now Jesus loved Martha, and her sister, and Lazarus. When he had heard therefore that he was sick, he abode two days still in the same place where he was. Then after that saith he to his disciples, Let us go into Judaea again.

His disciples say unto him, Master, the Jews of late sought to stone thee; and goest thou thither again?

Jesus answered, Are there not twelve hours in the day? If any man walk in the day, he stumbleth not, because he seeth the light of this world. But if a man walk in the night, he stumbleth, because there is no light in him. These things said he: and after that he saith unto them, Our friend Lazarus sleepeth; but I go, that I may awake him out of sleep.

Then said his disciples, Lord, if he sleep, he shall do well. Howbeit Jesus spake of his death: but they thought that he had spoken of taking of rest in sleep.

Then said Jesus unto them plainly, Lazarus is dead. And I am glad for your sakes that I was not there, to the intent ye may believe; nevertheless let us go unto him.

Then said Thomas, which is called Didymus, unto his fellowdisciples, Let us also go, that we may die with him.

Then when Jesus came, he found that he had lain in the grave four days already. Now Bethany was nigh unto Jerusalem, about fifteen furlongs off: And many of the Jews came to Martha and Mary, to comfort them concerning their brother.

Then Martha, as soon as she heard that Jesus was coming, went and met him: but Mary sat still in the house. Then said Martha unto Jesus, Lord, if thou hadst been here, my brother had not died. But I know, that even now, whatsoever thou wilt ask of God, God will give it thee.

Jesus saith unto her, Thy brother shall rise again.

Martha saith unto him, I know that he shall rise again in the resurrection at the last day.

Jesus said unto her, I am the resurrection, and the life: he that believeth in me, though he were dead, yet shall he live: And whosoever liveth and believeth in me shall never die. Believest thou this?

She saith unto him, Yea, Lord: I believe that thou art the Christ, the Son of God, which should come into the world.

And when she had so said, she went her way, and called Mary her sister secretly, saying, The Master is come, and calleth for thee. As soon as she heard that, she arose quickly, and came unto him. Now Jesus was not yet come into the town, but was in that place where Martha met him. The Jews then which were with her in the house, and comforted her, when they saw Mary, that she rose up hastily and went out, followed her, saying, She goeth unto the grave to weep there.

Then when Mary was come where Jesus was, and saw him, she fell down at his feet, saying unto him, Lord, if thou hadst been here, my brother had not died.

When Jesus therefore saw her weeping, and the Jews also weeping which came with her, he groaned in the spirit, and was troubled. And said, Where have ye laid him?

They said unto him, Lord, come and see.

Jesus wept. Then said the Jews, Behold how he loved him!

And some of them said, Could not this man, which opened the eyes of the blind, have caused that even this man should not have died?

Jesus therefore again groaning in himself cometh to the grave. It was a cave, and a stone lay upon it. Jesus said, Take ye away the stone.

Martha, the sister of him that was dead, saith unto him, Lord, by this time he stinketh: for he hath been dead four days.

Jesus saith unto her, Said I not unto thee, that, if thou wouldest believe, thou shouldest see the glory of God? Then they took away the stone from the place where the dead was laid. And Jesus lifted up his eyes, and said, Father, I thank thee that thou hast heard me. And I knew that thou hearest me always: but because of the people which stand by I said it, that they may believe that thou hast sent me. And when he thus had spoken, he cried with a loud voice, Lazarus, come forth. And he that was dead came forth, bound hand and foot with graveclothes: and his face was bound about with a napkin. Jesus saith unto them, Loose him, and let him go. (John 11:1–44)

---

*The sting of death is sin; and the strength of sin is the law. But thanks be to God, which giveth us the victory through our Lord Jesus Christ.*
*(1 Corinthians 15:56–57)*

HOW MARVELLOUS, HOW WONDERFUL IS MY SAVIOUR'S LOVE FOR ME

Thou hast turned for me my
mourning into dancing: thou hast
put off my sackcloth, and girded me
with gladness; To the end that my
glory may sing praise to thee, and
not be silent. O Lord my God, I
will give thanks unto thee for ever.

(Psalm 30:11–12)

# Thou art loosed from thine infirmity

And he was teaching in one of the synagogues on the sabbath. And, behold, there was a woman which had a spirit of infirmity eighteen years, and was bowed together, and could in no wise lift up herself. And when Jesus saw her, he called her to him, and said unto her, Woman, thou art loosed from thine infirmity. And he laid his hands on her: and immediately she was made straight, and glorified God.

And the ruler of the synagogue answered with indignation, because that Jesus had healed on the sabbath day, and said unto the people, There are six days in which men ought to work: in them therefore come and be healed, and not on the sabbath day.

The Lord then answered him, and said, Thou hypocrite, doth not each one of you on the sabbath loose his ox or his ass from the stall, and lead him away to watering? And ought not this woman, being a daughter of Abraham, whom Satan hath bound, lo, these eighteen years, be loosed from this bond on the sabbath day? And when he had said these things, all his adversaries were ashamed: and all the people rejoiced for all the glorious things that were done by him. (Luke 13:10–17)

---

*Many there be which say of my soul, There is no help for him in God.*
*But thou, O Lord, art a shield for me; my glory, and the lifter up of mine head.*
*(Psalm 3:2–3)*

# What therefore God hath joined together, let not man put asunder

And it came to pass, that when Jesus had finished these sayings, he departed from Galilee, and came into the coasts of Judaea beyond Jordan; And great multitudes followed him; and he healed them there.

The Pharisees also came unto him, tempting him, and saying unto him, Is it lawful for a man to put away his wife for every cause?

And he answered and said unto them, Have ye not read, that he which made them at the beginning made them male and female, And said, For this cause shall a man leave father and mother, and shall cleave to his wife: and they twain shall be one flesh? Wherefore they are no more twain, but one flesh. What therefore God hath joined together, let not man put asunder.

They say unto him, Why did Moses then command to give a writing of divorcement, and to put her away?

He saith unto them, Moses because of the hardness of your hearts suffered you to put away your wives: but from the beginning it was not so. And I say unto you, Whosoever shall put away his wife, except it be for fornication, and shall marry another, committeth adultery: and whoso marrieth her which is put away doth commit adultery.

His disciples say unto him, If the case of the man be so with his wife, it is not good to marry.

But he said unto them, All men cannot receive this saying, save they to whom it is given. For there are some eunuchs, which were so born from their mother's womb: and there are some eunuchs, which were made eunuchs of men: and there be eunuchs, which have made themselves eunuchs for the kingdom of heaven's sake. He that is able to receive it, let him receive it.
(Matthew 19:1–12)

*For this cause shall a man leave his father and mother, and shall be joined unto his wife, and they two shall be one flesh. This is a great mystery: but I speak concerning Christ and the church.*
*(Ephesians 5:31–32)*

ON CHRIST, THE SOLID ROCK, I STAND; ALL OTHER GROUND IS SINKING SAND

# For of such is the Kingdom of God

And they brought young children to him, that he should touch them: and his disciples rebuked those that brought them. But when Jesus saw it, he was much displeased, and said unto them, Suffer the little children to come unto me, and forbid them not: for of such is the kingdom of God. Verily I say unto you, Whosoever shall not receive the kingdom of God as a little child, he shall not enter therein. And he took them up in his arms, put his hands upon them, and blessed them.
(Mark 10:13–16)

*Take heed that ye despise not one of these little ones; for I say unto you, That in heaven their angels do always behold the face of my Father which is in heaven.*
*(Matthew 18:10)*

Verily I say unto you, Except ye be converted, and become as little children, ye shall not enter into the kingdom of heaven. Whosoever therefore shall humble himself as this little child, the same is greatest in the kingdom of heaven. And whoso shall receive one such little child in my name receiveth me.

(Matthew 18:3–5)

# And Jesus stood still

And they came to Jericho: and as he went out of Jericho with his disciples and a great number of people, blind Bartimaeus, the son of Timaeus, sat by the highway side begging. And when he heard that it was Jesus of Nazareth, he began to cry out, and say, Jesus, thou son of David, have mercy on me.

And many charged him that he should hold his peace: but he cried the more a great deal, Thou son of David, have mercy on me.

And Jesus stood still, and commanded him to be called.

And they call the blind man, saying unto him, Be of good comfort, rise; he calleth thee.

And he, casting away his garment, rose, and came to Jesus.

And Jesus answered and said unto him, What wilt thou that I should do unto thee?

The blind man said unto him, Lord, that I might receive my sight.

And Jesus said unto him, Go thy way; thy faith hath made thee whole. And immediately he received his sight, and followed Jesus in the way.
(Mark 10:46–52)

---

*I had fainted, unless I had believed to see the goodness of the Lord in the land of the living.*
*Wait on the Lord: be of good courage, and he shall strengthen thine heart: wait, I say, on the Lord.*
*(Psalm 27:13–14)*

# The Son of Man is come to seek and to save that which was lost

And Jesus entered and passed through Jericho. And, behold, there was a man named Zacchaeus, which was the chief among the publicans, and he was rich. And he sought to see Jesus who he was; and could not for the press, because he was little of stature. And he ran before, and climbed up into a sycomore tree to see him: for he was to pass that way. And when Jesus came to the place, he looked up, and saw him, and said unto him, Zacchaeus, make haste, and come down; for to day I must abide at thy house. And he made haste, and came down, and received him joyfully. And when they saw it, they all murmured, saying, That he was gone to be guest with a man that is a sinner.

And Zacchaeus stood, and said unto the Lord: Behold, Lord, the half of my goods I give to the poor; and if I have taken any thing from any man by false accusation, I restore him fourfold.

And Jesus said unto him, This day is salvation come to this house, forsomuch as he also is a son of Abraham. For the Son of man is come to seek and to save that which was lost.
(Luke 19:1–10)

*They that be whole need not a physician, but they that are sick. But go ye and learn what that meaneth, I will have mercy, and not sacrifice: for I am not come to call the righteous, but sinners to repentance.*
*(Matthew 9:12–13)*

# For the poor always ye have with you; but Me ye have not always

Then Jesus six days before the passover came to Bethany, where Lazarus was, which had been dead, whom he raised from the dead. There they made him a supper; and Martha served: but Lazarus was one of them that sat at the table with him. Then took Mary a pound of ointment of spikenard, very costly, and anointed the feet of Jesus, and wiped his feet with her hair: and the house was filled with the odour of the ointment.

Then saith one of his disciples, Judas Iscariot, Simon's son, which should betray him, Why was not this ointment sold for three hundred pence, and given to the poor? This he said, not that he cared for the poor; but because he was a thief, and had the bag, and bare what was put therein.

Then said Jesus, Let her alone: against the day of my burying hath she kept this. For the poor always ye have with you; but me ye have not always.

Much people of the Jews therefore knew that he was there: and they came not for Jesus' sake only, but that they might see Lazarus also, whom he had raised from the dead. But the chief priests consulted that they might put Lazarus also to death; Because that by reason of him many of the Jews went away, and believed on Jesus.
(John 12:1–11)

---

*And the men of Judah came, and there they anointed David king over the house of Judah.*
*(2 Samuel 2:4)*

NONE CAN BE NEARER, FAIRER, OR DEARER, THAN THOU MY SAVIOUR ART TO ME

# Hosanna in the highest

And it came to pass, when he was come nigh to Bethphage and Bethany, at the mount called the mount of Olives, he sent two of his disciples, Saying, Go ye into the village over against you; in the which at your entering ye shall find a colt tied, whereon yet never man sat: loose him, and bring him hither. And if any man ask you, Why do ye loose him? thus shall ye say unto him, Because the Lord hath need of him.

And they that were sent went their way, and found even as he had said unto them. And as they were loosing the colt, the owners thereof said unto them, Why loose ye the colt?

And they said, The Lord hath need of him. And they brought him to Jesus: and they cast their garments upon the colt, and they set Jesus thereon. And as he went, they spread their clothes in the way.

And when he was come nigh, even now at the descent of the mount of Olives, the whole multitude of the disciples began to rejoice and praise God with a loud voice for all the mighty works that they had seen; Saying,
Blessed be the King that cometh in the name of the Lord:
peace in heaven, and glory in the highest.

And some of the Pharisees from among the multitude said unto him, Master, rebuke thy disciples.

And he answered and said unto them, I tell you that, if these should hold their peace, the stones would immediately cry out.
(Luke 19:29–40)

*Rejoice greatly, O daughter of Zion; shout, O daughter of Jerusalem: behold, thy King cometh unto thee:*
*he is just, and having salvation; lowly, and riding upon an ass, and upon a colt the foal of an ass.*
*(Zechariah 9:9)*

*Know therefore and understand, that from the going forth of the commandment to restore and to build*
*Jerusalem unto the Messiah the Prince shall be seven weeks, and threescore and two weeks:*
*the street shall be built again, and the wall, even in troublous times.*
*(Daniel 9:25)*

# Because thou knewest not the time of thy visitation

And when he was come near, he beheld the city, and wept over it, Saying, If thou hadst known, even thou, at least in this thy day, the things which belong unto thy peace! but now they are hid from thine eyes. For the days shall come upon thee, that thine enemies shall cast a trench about thee, and compass thee round, and keep thee in on every side, And shall lay thee even with the ground, and thy children within thee; and they shall not leave in thee one stone upon another; because thou knewest not the time of thy visitation.
(Luke 19:41–44)

*O Jerusalem, Jerusalem, thou that killest the prophets, and stonest them which*
*are sent unto thee, how often would I have gathered thy children together,*
*even as a hen gathereth her chickens under her wings, and ye would not!*
*(Matthew 23:37)*

# Mine house shall be called an house of prayer

And Jesus entered into Jerusalem, and into the temple: and when he had looked round about upon all things, and now the eventide was come, he went out unto Bethany with the twelve.

And on the morrow, when they were come from Bethany, he was hungry: And seeing a fig tree afar off having leaves, he came, if haply he might find any thing thereon: and when he came to it, he found nothing but leaves; for the time of figs was not yet. And Jesus answered and said unto it, No man eat fruit of thee hereafter for ever.

And his disciples heard it.

And they come to Jerusalem: and Jesus went into the temple, and began to cast out them that sold and bought in the temple, and overthrew the tables of the moneychangers, and the seats of them that sold doves; And would not suffer that any man should carry any vessel through the temple. And he taught, saying unto them, Is it not written, My house shall be called of all nations the house of prayer? but ye have made it a den of thieves.

And the scribes and chief priests heard it, and sought how they might destroy him: for they feared him, because all the people was astonished at his doctrine. And when even was come, he went out of the city.
(Mark 11:11–19)

*Even them will I bring to my holy mountain, and make them joyful in my*
*house of prayer: their burnt offerings and their sacrifices shall be accepted upon*
*mine altar; for mine house shall be called an house of prayer for all people.*
*(Isaiah 56:7)*

# Have faith in God

And in the morning, as they passed by, they saw the fig tree dried up from the roots. And Peter calling to remembrance saith unto him, Master, behold, the fig tree which thou cursedst is withered away.

And Jesus answering saith unto them, Have faith in God. For verily I say unto you, That whosoever shall say unto this mountain, Be thou removed, and be thou cast into the sea; and shall not doubt in his heart, but shall believe that those things which he saith shall come to pass; he shall have whatsoever he saith. Therefore I say unto you, What things soever ye desire, when ye pray, believe that ye receive them, and ye shall have them.
(Mark 11:20–24)

---

*If ye abide in me, and my words abide in you, ye shall ask what ye will, and it shall be done*
*unto you. Herein is my Father glorified, that ye bear much fruit; so shall ye be my disciples.*
*(John 15:7–8)*

# Whose is this image and superscription?

Then went the Pharisees, and took counsel how they might entangle him in his talk. And they sent out unto him their disciples with the Herodians, saying, Master, we know that thou art true, and teachest the way of God in truth, neither carest thou for any man: for thou regardest not the person of men. Tell us therefore, What thinkest thou? Is it lawful to give tribute unto Caesar, or not?

But Jesus perceived their wickedness, and said, Why tempt ye me, ye hypocrites? Shew me the tribute money.

And they brought unto him a penny.

And he saith unto them, Whose is this image and superscription?

They say unto him, Caesar's.

Then saith he unto them, Render therefore unto Caesar the things which are Caesar's; and unto God the things that are God's. When they had heard these words, they marvelled, and left him, and went their way.
(Matthew 22:15–22)

---

*So God created man in his own image, in the image of*
*God created he him; male and female created he them.*
*(Genesis 1:27)*

# But she of her want did cast in all that she had

And Jesus sat over against the treasury, and beheld how the people cast money into the treasury: and many that were rich cast in much. And there came a certain poor widow, and she threw in two mites, which make a farthing. And he called unto him his disciples, and saith unto them, Verily I say unto you, That this poor widow hath cast more in, than all they which have cast into the treasury: For all they did cast in of their abundance; but she of her want did cast in all that she had, even all her living.
(Mark 12:41–44)

---

*And the king said unto Araunah, Nay; but I will surely buy it of thee at a price: neither will I offer burnt offerings unto the Lord my God of that which doth cost me nothing.*
*(2 Samuel 24:24)*

But this I say, He which soweth sparingly shall reap also sparingly; and he which soweth bountifully shall reap also bountifully. Every man according as he purposeth in his heart, so let him give; not grudgingly, or of necessity: for God loveth a cheerful giver. And God is able to make all grace abound toward you; that ye, always having all sufficiency in all things, may abound to every good work.

(2 Corinthians 9:6-8)

# Take ye heed, watch and pray

And as he went out of the temple, one of his disciples saith unto him, Master, see what manner of stones and what buildings are here!

And Jesus answering said unto him, Seest thou these great buildings? there shall not be left one stone upon another, that shall not be thrown down.

And as he sat upon the mount of Olives over against the temple, Peter and James and John and Andrew asked him privately, Tell us, when shall these things be? and what shall be the sign when all these things shall be fulfilled?

And Jesus answering them began to say, Take heed lest any man deceive you: For many shall come in my name, saying, I am Christ; and shall deceive many. And when ye shall hear of wars and rumours of wars, be ye not troubled: for such things must needs be; but the end shall not be yet. For nation shall rise against nation, and kingdom against kingdom: and there shall be earthquakes in divers places, and there shall be famines and troubles: these are the beginnings of sorrows.

But take heed to yourselves: for they shall deliver you up to councils; and in the synagogues ye shall be beaten: and ye shall be brought before rulers and kings for my sake, for a testimony against them. And the gospel must first be published among all nations. But when they shall lead you, and deliver you up, take no thought beforehand what ye shall speak, neither do ye premeditate: but whatsoever shall be given you in that hour, that speak ye: for it is not ye that speak, but the Holy Ghost. Now the brother shall betray the brother to death, and the father the son; and children shall rise up against their parents, and shall cause them to be put to death. And ye shall be hated of all men for my name's sake: but he that shall endure unto the end, the same shall be saved.

But when ye shall see the abomination of desolation, spoken of by Daniel the prophet, standing where it ought not, (let him that readeth understand,) then let them that be in Judaea flee to the mountains: And let him that is on the housetop not go down into the house, neither enter therein, to take any thing out of his house: And let him that is in the field not turn back again

for to take up his garment. But woe to them that are with child, and to them that give suck in those days! And pray ye that your flight be not in the winter. For in those days shall be affliction, such as was not from the beginning of the creation which God created unto this time, neither shall be. And except that the Lord had shortened those days, no flesh should be saved: but for the elect's sake, whom he hath chosen, he hath shortened the days.

And then if any man shall say to you, Lo, here is Christ; or, lo, he is there; believe him not: For false Christs and false prophets shall rise, and shall shew signs and wonders, to seduce, if it were possible, even the elect. But take ye heed: behold, I have foretold you all things.

But in those days, after that tribulation, the sun shall be darkened, and the moon shall not give her light, And the stars of heaven shall fall, and the powers that are in heaven shall be shaken. And then shall they see the Son of man coming in the clouds with great power and glory. And then shall he send his angels, and shall gather together his elect from the four winds, from the

uttermost part of the earth to the uttermost part of heaven.

Now learn a parable of the fig tree; When her branch is yet tender, and putteth forth leaves, ye know that summer is near: So ye in like manner, when ye shall see these things come to pass, know that it is nigh, even at the doors. Verily I say unto you, that this generation shall not pass, till all these things be done. Heaven and earth shall pass away: but my words shall not pass away.

But of that day and that hour knoweth no man, no, not the angels which are in heaven, neither the Son, but the Father. Take ye heed, watch and pray: for ye know not when the time is. For the Son of Man is as a man taking a far journey, who left his house, and gave authority to his servants, and to every man his work, and commanded the porter to watch. Watch ye therefore: for ye know not when the master of the house cometh, at even, or at midnight, or at the cockcrowing, or in the morning: Lest coming suddenly he find you sleeping. And what I say unto you I say unto all, Watch.
(Mark 13:1–37)

---

*For the Lord himself shall descend from heaven with a shout, with the voice of the archangel, and with the trump of God: and the dead in Christ shall rise first:*
*Then we which are alive and remain shall be caught up together with them in the clouds, to meet the Lord in the air: and so shall we ever be with the Lord.*
*(1 Thessalonians 4:16–17)*

# This also that she hath done shall be spoken of for a memorial of her

And being in Bethany in the house of Simon the leper, as he sat at meat, there came a woman having an alabaster box of ointment of spikenard very precious; and she brake the box, and poured it on his head. And there were some that had indignation within themselves, and said, Why was this waste of the ointment made? For it might have been sold for more than three hundred pence, and have been given to the poor. And they murmured against her.

And Jesus said, Let her alone; why trouble ye her? she hath wrought a good work on me. For ye have the poor with you always, and whensoever ye will ye may do them good: but me ye have not always. She hath done what she could: she is come aforehand to anoint my body to the burying. Verily I say unto you, Wheresoever this gospel shall be preached throughout the whole world, this also that she hath done shall be spoken of for a memorial of her.

And Judas Iscariot, one of the twelve, went unto the chief priests, to betray him unto them. And when they heard it, they were glad, and promised to give him money. And he sought how he might conveniently betray him.
(Mark 14:3–11)

---

*So all the elders of Israel came to the king to Hebron; and king David made a league*
*with them in Hebron before the Lord: and they anointed David king over Israel.*
*(2 Samuel 5:3)*

And the scribe said unto him, Well, Master, thou hast said the truth: for there is one God; and there is none other but he: And to love him with all the heart, and with all the understanding, and with all the soul, and with all the strength, and to love his neighbour as himself, is more than all whole burnt offerings and sacrifices. And when Jesus saw that he answered discreetly, he said unto him, Thou art not far from the kingdom of God.

(Mark 12:32–34)

# If I wash thee not, thou hast no part with Me

Now before the feast of the passover, when Jesus knew that his hour was come that he should depart out of this world unto the Father, having loved his own which were in the world, he loved them unto the end.

And supper being ended, the devil having now put into the heart of Judas Iscariot, Simon's son, to betray him; Jesus knowing that the Father had given all things into his hands, and that he was come from God, and went to God; He riseth from supper, and laid aside his garments; and took a towel, and girded himself. After that he poureth water into a bason, and began to wash the disciples' feet, and to wipe them with the towel wherewith he was girded. Then cometh he to Simon Peter: and Peter saith unto him, Lord, dost thou wash my feet?

Jesus answered and said unto him, What I do thou knowest not now; but thou shalt know hereafter.

Peter saith unto him, Thou shalt never wash my feet.

Jesus answered him, If I wash thee not, thou hast no part with me.

Simon Peter saith unto him, Lord, not my feet only, but also my hands and my head.

Jesus saith to him, He that is washed needeth not save to wash his feet, but is clean every whit: and ye are clean, but not all. For he knew who should betray him; therefore said he, Ye are not all clean.

So after he had washed their feet, and had taken his garments, and was set down again, he said unto them, Know ye what I have done to you? Ye call me Master and Lord: and ye say well; for so I am. If I then, your Lord and Master, have washed your feet; ye also ought to wash one another's feet. For I have given you an example, that ye should do as I have done to you. Verily, verily, I say unto you, The servant is not greater than his lord; neither he that is sent greater than he that sent him. If ye know these things, happy are ye if ye do them.
(John 13:1–17)

---

*For whether is greater, he that sitteth at meat, or he that serveth? is not he that sitteth at meat? but I am among you as he that serveth.*
*(Luke 22:27)*

A new commandment I give
unto you, That ye love one
another; as I have loved you,
that ye also love one another.
By this shall all men know
that ye are my disciples, if ye
have love one to another.

(John 13:34-35)

# This do in remembrance of Me

And as they did eat, he said, Verily I say unto you, that one of you shall betray me.

And they were exceeding sorrowful, and began every one of them to say unto him, Lord, is it I?

And he answered and said, He that dippeth his hand with me in the dish, the same shall betray me. The Son of man goeth as it is written of him: but woe unto that man by whom the Son of man is betrayed! it had been good for that man if he had not been born.

Then Judas, which betrayed him, answered and said, Master, is it I?

He said unto him, Thou hast said.

And as they were eating, Jesus took bread, and blessed it, and brake it, and gave it to the disciples, and said, Take, eat; this is my body.

And he took the cup, and gave thanks, and gave it to them, saying, Drink ye all of it; For this is my blood of the new testament, which is shed for many for the remission of sins.

But I say unto you, I will not drink henceforth of this fruit of the vine, until that day when I drink it new with you in my Father's kingdom.
(Matthew 26:21–29)

These words spake Jesus, and lifted up his eyes to heaven, and said, Father, the hour is come; glorify thy Son, that thy Son also may glorify thee: As thou hast given him power over all flesh, that he should give eternal life to as many as thou hast given him. And this is life eternal, that they might know thee the only true God, and Jesus Christ, whom thou hast sent. I have glorified thee on the earth: I have finished the work which thou gavest me to do. And now, O Father, glorify thou me with thine own self with the glory which I had with thee before the world was.

I have manifested thy name unto the men which thou gavest me out of the world: thine they were, and thou gavest them me; and they have kept thy word. Now they have known that all things whatsoever thou hast given me are of thee. For I have given unto them the words which thou gavest me; and they have received them, and have known surely that I came out from thee, and they have believed that thou didst send me.

I pray for them: I pray not for the world, but for them which thou hast given me; for they are thine. And all mine are thine, and thine are mine; and I am glorified in them. And now I am no more in the world, but these are in the world, and I come to thee. Holy Father, keep through thine own name those whom thou hast given me, that they may be one, as we are. While I was with them in the world, I kept them in thy name: those that thou gavest me I have kept, and none of them is lost, but the son of perdition; that the scripture might be fulfilled. And now come I to thee; and these things I speak in the world, that they might have my joy fulfilled in themselves. I have given them thy word; and the world hath hated them, because they are not of the world, even as I am not of the world. I pray not that thou shouldest take them out of the world, but that thou shouldest keep them from the evil. They are not of the world, even as I am not of the world. Sanctify them through thy truth: thy word is truth. As thou hast sent me into the world, even so have I also sent them into the world. And for their sakes I sanctify myself, that they also might be sanctified through the truth.

Neither pray I for these alone, but for them also which shall believe on me through their word; That they all may be one; as thou, Father, art in me, and I in thee, that they also may be one in us: that the world may believe that thou hast sent me. And the glory which thou gavest me I have given them; that they may be one, even as we are one: I in them, and thou in me, that they may be made perfect in one; and that the world may know that thou hast sent me, and hast loved them, as thou hast loved me.

Father, I will that they also, whom thou hast given me, be with me where I am; that they may behold my glory, which thou hast given me: for thou lovedst me before the foundation of the world. O righteous Father, the world hath not known thee: but I have known thee, and these have known that thou hast sent me. And I have declared unto them thy name, and will declare it: that the love wherewith thou hast loved me may be in them, and I in them.
(John 17:1–26)

*These things I have spoken unto you, that in me ye might have peace. In the world ye shall have tribulation: but be of good cheer; I have overcome the world.*
*(John 16:33)*

# Not My will, but Thine, be done

And when they had sung an hymn, they went out into the mount of Olives.

Then saith Jesus unto them, All ye shall be offended because of me this night: for it is written,
I will smite the shepherd,
and the sheep of the flock shall be scattered abroad.

But after I am risen again, I will go before you into Galilee.

Peter answered and said unto him, Though all men shall be offended because of thee, yet will I never be offended.

Jesus said unto him, Verily I say unto thee, That this night, before the cock crow, thou shalt deny me thrice.

Peter said unto him, Though I should die with thee, yet will I not deny thee.

Likewise also said all the disciples.

Then cometh Jesus with them unto a place called Gethsemane, and saith unto the disciples, Sit ye here, while I go and pray yonder. And he took with him Peter and the two sons of Zebedee, and began to be sorrowful and very heavy. Then saith he unto them, My soul is exceeding sorrowful, even unto death: tarry ye here, and watch with me.

And he went a little farther, and fell on his face, and prayed, saying, O my Father, if it be possible, let this cup pass from me: nevertheless not as I will, but as thou wilt.

And he cometh unto the disciples, and findeth them asleep, and saith unto Peter, What, could ye not watch with me one hour? Watch and pray, that ye enter not into temptation: the spirit indeed is willing, but the flesh is weak.

He went away again the second time, and prayed, saying, O my Father, if this cup may not pass away from me, except I drink it, thy will be done.

And he came and found them asleep again: for their eyes were heavy.

And he left them, and went away again, and prayed the third time, saying the same words. Then cometh he to his disciples, and saith unto them, Sleep on now, and take your rest: behold, the hour is at hand, and the Son of man is betrayed into the hands of sinners. Rise, let us be going: behold, he is at hand that doth betray me.
(Matthew 26:30–46)

---

*And being in an agony he prayed more earnestly: and his sweat was as it were great drops of blood falling down to the ground.*
*(Luke 22:44)*

*Now is my soul troubled; and what shall I say? Father, save me from this hour: but for this cause came I unto this hour.*
*(John 12:27)*

LOOK ON THE HEART BY SORROW BROKEN, LOOK ON THE TEARS BY SINNERS SHED

Who in the days of his flesh, when he had offered up prayers and supplications with strong crying and tears unto him that was able to save him from death, and was heard in that he feared; Though he were a Son, yet learned he obedience by the things which he suffered; And being made perfect, he became the author of eternal salvation unto all them that obey him; Called of God an high priest after the order of Melchisedec.

(Hebrews 5:7-10)

# Betrayest thou the Son of Man with a kiss?

And immediately, while he yet spake, cometh Judas, one of the twelve, and with him a great multitude with swords and staves, from the chief priests and the scribes and the elders. And he that betrayed him had given them a token, saying, Whomsoever I shall kiss, that same is he; take him, and lead him away safely.

And as soon as he was come, he goeth straightway to him, and saith, Master, master; and kissed him. (Mark 14:43–45)

---

*Yea, mine own familiar friend, in whom I trusted, which did*
*eat of my bread, hath lifted up his heel against me.*
*(Psalm 41:9)*

# I am

Jesus therefore, knowing all things that should come upon him, went forth, and said unto them, Whom seek ye?

They answered him, Jesus of Nazareth. Jesus saith unto them, I am he. And Judas also, which betrayed him, stood with them. As soon then as he had said unto them, I am he, they went backward, and fell to the ground.

Then asked he them again, Whom seek ye?

And they said, Jesus of Nazareth.

Jesus answered, I have told you that I am he: if therefore ye seek me, let these go their way: That the saying might be fulfilled, which he spake, Of them which thou gavest me have I lost none.

Then Simon Peter having a sword drew it, and smote the high priest's servant, and cut off his right ear. The servant's name was Malchus.

Then said Jesus unto Peter, Put up thy sword into the sheath: the cup which my Father hath given me, shall I not drink it?
(John 18:4–11)

And he touched his ear, and healed him.

Then Jesus said unto the chief priests, and captains of the temple, and the elders, which were come to him, Be ye come out, as against a thief, with swords and staves? When I was daily with you in the temple, ye stretched forth no hands against me: but this is your hour, and the power of darkness.
(Luke 22:51–53)

---

*Therefore doth my Father love me, because I lay down my life, that I might take it again.*
*No man taketh it from me, but I lay it down of myself. I have power to lay it down, and*
*I have power to take it again. This commandment have I received of my Father.*
*(John 10:17–18)*

# And the Lord turned, and looked upon Peter

Then the band and the captain and officers of the Jews took Jesus, and bound him, And led him away to Annas first; for he was father in law to Caiaphas, which was the high priest that same year. Now Caiaphas was he, which gave counsel to the Jews, that it was expedient that one man should die for the people.

And Simon Peter followed Jesus, and so did another disciple: that disciple was known unto the high priest, and went in with Jesus into the palace of the high priest. But Peter stood at the door without. Then went out that other disciple, which was known unto the high priest, and spake unto her that kept the door, and brought in Peter. Then saith the damsel that kept the door unto Peter, Art not thou also one of this man's disciples?

He saith, I am not.

And the servants and officers stood there, who had made a fire of coals; for it was cold: and they warmed themselves: and Peter stood with them, and warmed himself.

The high priest then asked Jesus of his disciples, and of his doctrine.

Jesus answered him, I spake openly to the world; I ever taught in the synagogue, and in the temple, whither the Jews always resort; and in secret have I said nothing. Why askest thou me? ask them which heard me, what I have said unto them: behold, they know what I said.

And when he had thus spoken, one of the officers which stood by struck Jesus with the palm of his hand, saying, Answerest thou the high priest so?

Jesus answered him, If I have spoken evil, bear witness of the evil: but if well, why smitest thou me?

Now Annas had sent him bound unto Caiaphas the high priest.

And Simon Peter stood and warmed himself. They said therefore unto him, Art not thou also one of his disciples?

He denied it, and said, I am not.

One of the servants of the high priest, being his kinsman whose ear Peter cut off, saith, Did not I see thee in the garden with him? Peter then denied again: and immediately the cock crew.
(John 18:12–27)

And the Lord turned, and looked upon Peter. And Peter remembered the word of the Lord, how he had said unto him, Before the cock crow, thou shalt deny me thrice. And Peter went out, and wept bitterly.
(Luke 22:61–62)

---

*And the Lord said, Simon, Simon, behold, Satan hath desired to have you, that he may sift you as wheat:*
*But I have prayed for thee, that thy faith fail not: and when thou art converted, strengthen thy brethren.*
*(Luke 22:31–32)*

# Many bare false witness against Him

And the chief priests and all the council sought for witness against Jesus to put him to death; and found none. For many bare false witness against him, but their witness agreed not together.

And there arose certain, and bare false witness against him, saying, We heard him say, I will destroy this temple that is made with hands, and within three days I will build another made without hands. But neither so did their witness agree together.

And the high priest stood up in the midst, and asked Jesus, saying, Answerest thou nothing? what is it which these witness against thee? But he held his peace, and answered nothing.

Again the high priest asked him, and said unto him, Art thou the Christ, the Son of the Blessed?

And Jesus said, I am: and ye shall see the Son of man sitting on the right hand of power, and coming in the clouds of heaven.

Then the high priest rent his clothes, and saith, What need we any further witnesses? Ye have heard the blasphemy: what think ye?

And they all condemned him to be guilty of death.

And some began to spit on him, and to cover his face, and to buffet him, and to say unto him, Prophesy: and the servants did strike him with the palms of their hands.
(Mark 14:55–65)

When the morning was come, all the chief priests and elders of the people took counsel against Jesus to put him to death: And when they had bound him, they led him away, and delivered him to Pontius Pilate the governor.
(Matthew 27:1–2)

---

*Behold, we go up to Jerusalem; and the Son of man shall be delivered unto the chief priests, and unto the scribes; and they shall condemn him to death, and shall deliver him to the Gentiles: And they shall mock him, and shall scourge him, and shall spit upon him, and shall kill him: and the third day he shall rise again.*
*(Mark 10:33–34)*

If therefore perfection were by the Levitical priesthood, (for under it the people received the law,) what further need was there that another priest should rise after the order of Melchisedec, and not be called after the order of Aaron? For the priesthood being changed, there is made of necessity a change also of the law. For he of whom these things are spoken pertaineth to another tribe, of which no man gave attendance at the altar. For it is evident that our Lord sprang out of Juda; of which tribe Moses spake nothing concerning priesthood. And it is yet far more evident: for that after the similitude of Melchisedec there ariseth another priest, Who is made, not after the law of a carnal commandment, but after the power of an endless life.

(Hebrews 7:11–16)

# Every one that is of the truth heareth My voice

Then led they Jesus from Caiaphas unto the hall of judgment: and it was early; and they themselves went not into the judgment hall, lest they should be defiled; but that they might eat the passover. Pilate then went out unto them, and said, What accusation bring ye against this man?

They answered and said unto him, If he were not a malefactor, we would not have delivered him up unto thee.

Then said Pilate unto them, Take ye him, and judge him according to your law.

The Jews therefore said unto him, It is not lawful for us to put any man to death: That the saying of Jesus might be fulfilled, which he spake, signifying what death he should die.

Then Pilate entered into the judgment hall again, and called Jesus, and said unto him, Art thou the King of the Jews?

Jesus answered him, Sayest thou this thing of thyself, or did others tell it thee of me?

Pilate answered, Am I a Jew? Thine own nation and the chief priests have delivered thee unto me: what hast thou done?

Jesus answered, My kingdom is not of this world: if my kingdom were of this world, then would my servants fight, that I should not be delivered to the Jews: but now is my kingdom not from hence.

Pilate therefore said unto him, Art thou a king then? Jesus answered, Thou sayest that I am a king. To this end was I born, and for this cause came I into the world, that I should bear witness unto the truth. Every one that is of the truth heareth my voice.

Pilate saith unto him, What is truth? And when he had said this, he went out again unto the Jews, and saith unto them, I find in him no fault at all. (John 18:28–38)

*For even hereunto were ye called: because Christ also suffered for us, leaving us an example, that ye should follow his steps: Who did no sin, neither was guile found in his mouth: Who, when he was reviled, reviled not again; when he suffered, he threatened not; but committed himself to him that judgeth righteously: Who his own self bare our sins in his own body on the tree, that we, being dead to sins, should live unto righteousness: by whose stripes ye were healed.*
*(1 Peter 2:21–24)*

# But He answered him nothing

And they were the more fierce, saying, He stirreth up the people, teaching throughout all Jewry, beginning from Galilee to this place.

When Pilate heard of Galilee, he asked whether the man were a Galilaean. And as soon as he knew that he belonged unto Herod's jurisdiction, he sent him to Herod, who himself also was at Jerusalem at that time. And when Herod saw Jesus, he was exceeding glad: for he was desirous to see him of a long season, because he had heard many things of him; and he hoped to have seen some miracle done by him. Then he questioned with him in many words; but he answered him nothing. And the chief priests and scribes stood and vehemently accused him. And Herod with his men of war set him at nought, and mocked him, and arrayed him in a gorgeous robe, and sent him again to Pilate. And the same day Pilate and Herod were made friends together: for before they were at enmity between themselves. (Luke 23:5–12)

---

*He was oppressed, and he was afflicted, yet he opened not his mouth: he is brought as a lamb*
*to the slaughter, and as a sheep before her shearers is dumb, so he openeth not his mouth.*
*(Isaiah 53:7)*

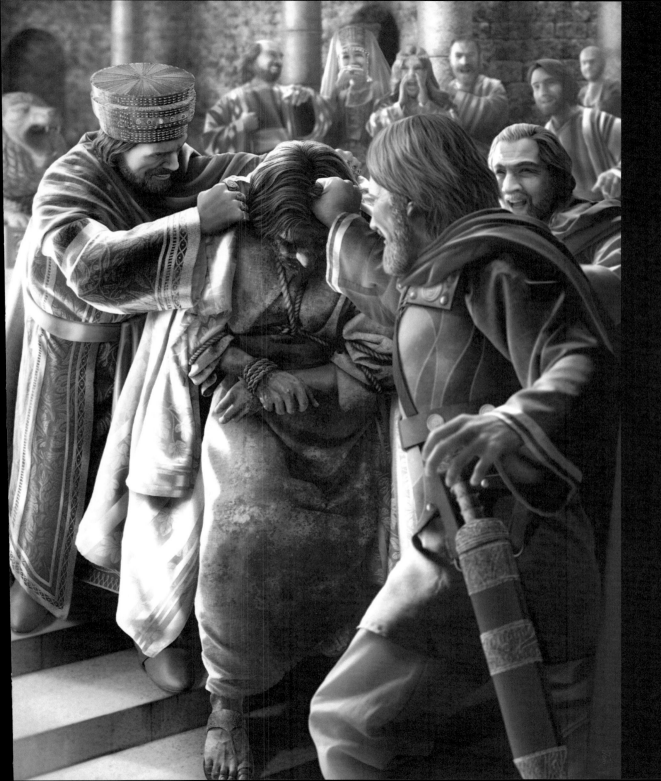

Looking unto Jesus the author and finisher of our faith; who for the joy that was set before him endured the cross, despising the shame, and is set down at the right hand of the throne of God. For consider him that endured such contradiction of sinners against himself, lest ye be wearied and faint in your minds.

(Hebrews 12:2–3)

# I find no fault in this Man

And Pilate, when he had called together the chief priests and the rulers and the people, Said unto them, Ye have brought this man unto me, as one that perverteth the people: and, behold, I, having examined him before you, have found no fault in this man touching those things whereof ye accuse him: No, nor yet Herod: for I sent you to him; and, lo, nothing worthy of death is done unto him. I will therefore chastise him, and release him. (For of necessity he must release one unto them at the feast.)
(Luke 23:13–17)

Now at that feast the governor was wont to release unto the people a prisoner, whom they would. And they had then a notable prisoner, called Barabbas. Therefore when they were gathered together, Pilate said unto them, Whom will ye that I release unto you? Barabbas, or Jesus which is called Christ? For he knew that for envy they had delivered him.

When he was set down on the judgment seat, his wife sent unto him, saying, Have thou nothing to do with that just man: for I have suffered many things this day in a dream because of him.

But the chief priests and elders persuaded the multitude that they should ask Barabbas, and destroy Jesus. The governor answered and said unto them, Whether of the twain will ye that I release unto you?

They said, Barabbas.

Pilate saith unto them, What shall I do then with Jesus which is called Christ?

They all say unto him, Let him be crucified.

And the governor said, Why, what evil hath he done?

But they cried out the more, saying, Let him be crucified.

When Pilate saw that he could prevail nothing, but that rather a tumult was made, he took water, and washed his hands before the multitude, saying, I am innocent of the blood of this just person: see ye to it.

Then answered all the people, and said, His blood be on us, and on our children.

Then released he Barabbas unto them: and when he had scourged Jesus, he delivered him to be crucified.
(Matthew 27:15–26)

---

*But not as the offence, so also is the free gift. For if through the offence of one many be dead, much more the grace of God, and the gift by grace, which is by one man, Jesus Christ, hath abounded unto many. And not as it was by one that sinned, so is the gift: for the judgment was by one to condemnation, but the free gift is of many offences unto justification. For if by one man's offence death reigned by one; much more they which receive abundance of grace and of the gift of righteousness shall reign in life by one, Jesus Christ.*
*(Romans 5:15–17)*

For when we were yet without strength, in due time Christ died for the ungodly. For scarcely for a righteous man will one die: yet peradventure for a good man some would even dare to die. But God commendeth his love toward us, in that, while we were yet sinners, Christ died for us. Much more then, being now justified by his blood, we shall be saved from wrath through him. For if, when we were enemies, we were reconciled to God by the death of his Son, much more, being reconciled, we shall be saved by his life.

(Romans 5:6-10)

# The plowers plowed upon my back: they made long their furrows

Then Pilate therefore took Jesus, and scourged him.
(John 19:1)

*He was taken from prison and from judgment: and who shall declare his generation? for he*
*was cut off out of the land of the living: for the transgression of my people was he stricken.*
*(Isaiah 53:8)*

Surely he hath borne our griefs, and
carried our sorrows: yet we did esteem him
stricken, smitten of God, and afflicted.
But he was wounded for our transgressions,
he was bruised for our iniquities: the
chastisement of our peace was upon him;
and with his stripes we are healed.

(Isaiah 53:4–5)

# And they bowed the knee before Him, and mocked Him

Then the soldiers of the governor took Jesus into the common hall, and gathered unto him the whole band of soldiers. And they stripped him, and put on him a scarlet robe. And when they had platted a crown of thorns, they put it upon his head, and a reed in his right hand: and they bowed the knee before him, and mocked him, saying, Hail, King of the Jews! (Matthew 27:27–29)

*For it became him, for whom are all things, and by whom are all things, in bringing many sons unto glory, to make the captain of their salvation perfect through sufferings.*
*(Hebrews 2:10)*

Yet it pleased the Lord to bruise him; he hath put him to grief: when thou shalt make his soul an offering for sin, he shall see his seed, he shall prolong his days, and the pleasure of the Lord shall prosper in his hand. He shall see of the travail of his soul, and shall be satisfied: by his knowledge shall my righteous servant justify many; for he shall bear their iniquities.

(Isaiah 53:10–11)

# I gave My back to the smiters, and My cheeks to them that plucked off the hair: I hid not My face from shame and spitting

And they spit upon him, and took the reed, and smote him on the head. And after that they had mocked him, they took the robe off from him, and put his own raiment on him, and led him away to crucify him. (Matthew 27:30–31)

*But that the world may know that I love the Father;*
*and as the Father gave me commandment, even so I do.*
*(John 14:31)*

# Weep not for Me

And as they led him away, they laid hold upon one Simon, a Cyrenian, coming out of the country, and on him they laid the cross, that he might bear it after Jesus.

And there followed him a great company of people, and of women, which also bewailed and lamented him. But Jesus turning unto them said, Daughters of Jerusalem, weep not for me, but weep for yourselves, and for your children. For, behold, the days are coming, in the which they shall say, Blessed are the barren, and the wombs that never bare, and the paps which never gave suck. Then shall they begin to say to the mountains, Fall on us; and to the hills, Cover us. For if they do these things in a green tree, what shall be done in the dry?
(Luke 23:26–31)

---

*And being found in fashion as a man, he humbled himself,*
*and became obedient unto death, even the death of the cross.*
*(Philippians 2:8)*

# *Father, forgive them;*
# for they know not what they do

And there were also two other, malefactors, led with him to be put to death. And when they were come to the place, which is called Calvary, there they crucified him, and the malefactors, one on the right hand, and the other on the left. Then said Jesus, Father, forgive them; for they know not what they do.

And they parted his raiment, and cast lots. And the people stood beholding. And the rulers also with them derided him, saying, He saved others; let him save himself, if he be Christ, the chosen of God.

And the soldiers also mocked him, coming to him, and offering him vinegar, And saying, If thou be the king of the Jews, save thyself.
(Luke 23:32–37)

*He is despised and rejected of men; a man of sorrows, and acquainted with grief:*
*and we hid as it were our faces from him; he was despised, and we esteemed him not.*
*(Isaiah 53:3)*

*For he hath made him to be sin for us, who knew no sin;*
*that we might be made the righteousness of God in him.*
*(2 Corinthians 5:21)*

For God so loved the world, that he gave his only begotten Son, that whosoever believeth in him should not perish, but have everlasting life. For God sent not his Son into the world to condemn the world; but that the world through him might be saved.

(John 3:16–17)

# Jesus of Nazareth, the King of the Jews

And Pilate wrote a title, and put it on the cross. And the writing was JESUS OF NAZARETH THE KING OF THE JEWS.

This title then read many of the Jews: for the place where Jesus was crucified was nigh to the city: and it was written in Hebrew, and Greek, and Latin.

Then said the chief priests of the Jews to Pilate, Write not, The King of the Jews; but that he said, I am King of the Jews.

Pilate answered, What I have written I have written.

Then the soldiers, when they had crucified Jesus, took his garments, and made four parts, to every soldier a part; and also his coat: now the coat was without seam, woven from the top throughout. They said therefore among themselves, Let us not rend it, but cast lots for it, whose it shall be: that the scripture might be fulfilled, which saith,

They parted my raiment among them,
and for my vesture they did cast lots.

These things therefore the soldiers did.

Now there stood by the cross of Jesus his mother, and his mother's sister, Mary the wife of Cleophas, and Mary Magdalene. When Jesus therefore saw his mother, and the disciple standing by, whom he loved, he saith unto his mother, Woman, behold thy son! Then saith he to the disciple, Behold thy mother! And from that hour that disciple took her unto his own home.
(John 19:19–27)

*And you, being dead in your sins and the uncircumcision of your flesh, hath he quickened together with him, having forgiven you all trespasses; Blotting out the handwriting of ordinances that was against us, which was contrary to us, and took it out of the way, nailing it to his cross; And having spoiled principalities and powers, he made a shew of them openly, triumphing over them in it.*
*(Colossians 2:13–15)*

*All we like sheep have gone astray; we have turned every one to his own way; and the Lord hath laid on him the iniquity of us all.*
*(Isaiah 53:6)*

*As far as the east is from the west, so far hath he removed our transgressions from us.*
*(Psalm 103:12)*

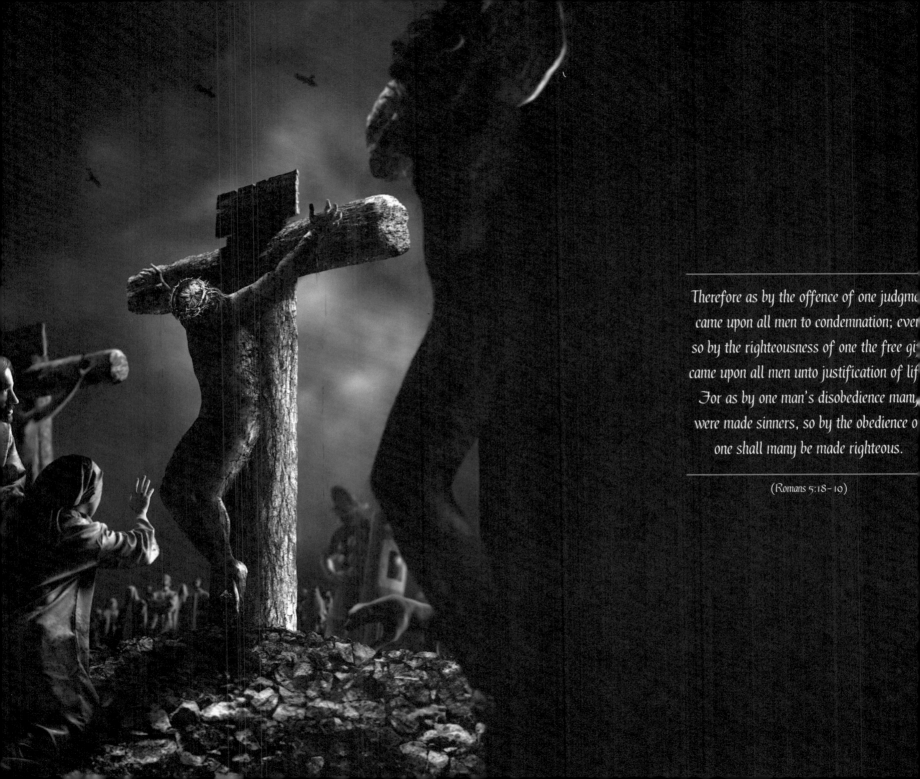

Therefore as by the offence of one judgme[nt]
came upon all men to condemnation; even
so by the righteousness of one the free gi[ft]
came upon all men unto justification of lif[e].
For as by one man's disobedience many,
were made sinners, so by the obedience o[f]
one shall many be made righteous.

(Romans 5:18–19)

# It is finished

Now from the sixth hour there was darkness over all the land unto the ninth hour. And about the ninth hour Jesus cried with a loud voice, saying, Eli, Eli, lama sabachthani? that is to say, My God, my God, why hast thou forsaken me?

Some of them that stood there, when they heard that, said, This man calleth for Elias. And straightway one of them ran, and took a spunge, and filled it with vinegar, and put it on a reed, and gave him to drink.

The rest said, Let be, let us see whether Elias will come to save him.

Jesus, when he had cried again with a loud voice, yielded up the ghost.
(Matthew 27:45–50)

---

*Christ hath redeemed us from the curse of the law, being made a curse for us: for it is written,*
*Cursed is every one that hangeth on a tree: That the blessing of Abraham might come on the*
*Gentiles through Jesus Christ; that we might receive the promise of the Spirit through faith.*
*(Galatians 3:13–14)*

*I am poured out like water, and all my bones are out of joint: my heart is like wax; it is*
*melted in the midst of my bowels. My strength is dried up like a potsherd; and my tongue*
*cleaveth to my jaws; and thou hast brought me into the dust of death. For dogs have*
*compassed me: the assembly of the wicked have inclosed me: they pierced my hands*
*and my feet. I may tell all my bones: they look and stare upon me.*
*(Psalm 22:14–17)*

*As many were astonied at thee; his visage was so marred*
*more than any man, and his form more than the sons of men.*
*(Isaiah 52:14)*

# They shall look on Him whom they pierced

The Jews therefore, because it was the preparation, that the bodies should not remain upon the cross on the sabbath day, (for that sabbath day was an high day,) besought Pilate that their legs might be broken, and that they might be taken away. Then came the soldiers, and brake the legs of the first, and of the other which was crucified with him. But when they came to Jesus, and saw that he was dead already, they brake not his legs: But one of the soldiers with a spear pierced his side, and forthwith came there out blood and water. And he that saw it bare record, and his record is true: and he knoweth that he saith true, that ye might believe. For these things were done, that the scripture should be fulfilled, A bone of him shall not be broken. And again another scripture saith, They shall look on him whom they pierced. (John 19:31–37)

*Be it known unto you therefore, men and brethren, that through this man ispreached*
*unto you the forgiveness of sins: And by him all that believe are justified from all*
*things, from which ye could not be justified by the law of Moses.*
*(Acts 13:38–39)*

*And after threescore and two weeks shall Messiah be cut off, but not for himself.*
*(Daniel 9:26)*

# The veil of the temple was rent in twain

And, behold, the veil of the temple was rent in twain from the top to the bottom; and the earth did quake, and the rocks rent; And the graves were opened; and many bodies of the saints which slept arose, And came out of the graves after his resurrection, and went into the holy city, and appeared unto many.

Now when the centurion, and they that were with him, watching Jesus, saw the earthquake, and those things that were done, they feared greatly, saying, Truly this was the Son of God.

And many women were there beholding afar off, which followed Jesus from Galilee, ministering unto him: Among which was Mary Magdalene, and Mary the mother of James and Joses, and the mother of Zebedees children. (Matthew 27:51–56)

---

*But Christ being come an high priest of good things to come, by a greater and more perfect tabernacle, not made with hands, that is to say, not of this building; Neither by the blood of goats and calves, but by his own blood he entered in once into the holy place, having obtained eternal redemption for us.*
*(Hebrews 9:11–12)*

# A new sepulchre, wherein was never man yet laid

When the even was come, there came a rich man of Arimathaea, named Joseph, who also himself was Jesus' disciple: He went to Pilate, and begged the body of Jesus. Then Pilate commanded the body to be delivered. And when Joseph had taken the body, he wrapped it in a clean linen cloth, And laid it in his own new tomb, which he had hewn out in the rock: and he rolled a great stone to the door of the sepulchre, and departed. And there was Mary Magdalene, and the other Mary, sitting over against the sepulchre.

Now the next day, that followed the day of the preparation, the chief priests and Pharisees came together unto Pilate, Saying, Sir, we remember that that deceiver said, while he was yet alive, After three days I will rise again. Command therefore that the sepulchre be made sure until the third day, lest his disciples come by night, and steal him away, and say unto the people, He is risen from the dead: so the last error shall be worse than the first.

Pilate said unto them, Ye have a watch: go your way, make it as sure as ye can. So they went, and made the sepulchre sure, sealing the stone, and setting a watch.
(Matthew 27:57–66)

---

*And he made his grave with the wicked, and with the rich in his death;*
*because he had done no violence, neither was any deceit in his mouth.*
*(Isaiah 53:9)*

*Verily, verily, I say unto you, Except a corn of wheat fall into the ground*
*and die, it abideth alone: but if it die, it bringeth forth much fruit.*
*(John 12:24)*

*For Christ also hath once suffered for sins, the just for the unjust, that he might bring us to God,*
*being put to death in the flesh, but quickened by the Spirit: By which also he went and preached unto*
*the spirits in prison; Which sometime were disobedient, when once the longsuffering of God waited in*
*the days of Noah, while the ark was a preparing, wherein few, that is, eight souls were saved by water.*
*(1 Peter 3:18–20)*

*For David speaketh concerning him, I foresaw the Lord always before my face, for he is on my right hand, that
I should not be moved: Therefore did my heart rejoice, and my tongue was glad; moreover also my flesh shall rest
in hope: Because thou wilt not leave my soul in hell, neither wilt thou suffer thine Holy One to see corruption.
Thou hast made known to me the ways of life; thou shalt make me full of joy with thy countenance. Men and
brethren, let me freely speak unto you of the patriarch David, that he is both dead and buried, and his sepulchre
is with us unto this day. Therefore being a prophet, and knowing that God had sworn with an oath to him, that
of the fruit of his loins, according to the flesh, he would raise up Christ to sit on his throne; He seeing this before
spake of the resurrection of Christ, that his soul was not left in hell, neither his flesh did see corruption.*
*(Acts 2:25–31)*

# They found the stone rolled away from the sepulchre

In the end of the sabbath, as it began to dawn toward the first day of the week, came Mary Magdalene and the other Mary to see the sepulchre. And, behold, there was a great earthquake: for the angel of the Lord descended from heaven, and came and rolled back the stone from the door, and sat upon it. His countenance was like lightning, and his raiment white as snow: And for fear of him the keepers did shake, and became as dead men.

And the angel answered and said unto the women, Fear not ye: for I know that ye seek Jesus, which was crucified. He is not here: for he is risen, as he said. Come, see the place where the Lord lay. And go quickly, and tell his disciples that he is risen from the dead; and, behold, he goeth before you into Galilee; there shall ye see him: lo, I have told you.

And they departed quickly from the sepulchre with fear and great joy; and did run to bring his disciples word. (Matthew 28:1–8)

---

*Knowing that Christ being raised from the dead dieth no more; death hath no more dominion over him.*
*(Romans 6:9)*

*Therefore will I divide him a portion with the great, and he shall divide the spoil with the strong; because he hath poured out his soul unto death: and he was numbered with the transgressors; and he bare the sin of many, and made intercession for the transgressors.*
*(Isaiah 53:12)*

# He is not here; for He is risen

Peter therefore went forth, and that other disciple, and came to the sepulchre. So they ran both together: and the other disciple did outrun Peter, and came first to the sepulchre. And he stooping down, and looking in, saw the linen clothes lying; yet went he not in. Then cometh Simon Peter following him, and went into the sepulchre, and seeth the linen clothes lie, And the napkin, that was about his head, not lying with the linen clothes, but wrapped together in a place by itself. Then went in also that other disciple, which came first to the sepulchre, and he saw, and believed. For as yet they knew not the scripture, that he must rise again from the dead. Then the disciples went away again unto their own home.
(John 20:3–10)

*For in that he died, he died unto sin once: but in that he liveth, he liveth unto God. Likewise reckon*
*ye also yourselves to be dead indeed unto sin, but alive unto God through Jesus Christ our Lord.*
*(Romans 6:10–11)*

# I ascend unto My Father, and your Father

But Mary stood without at the sepulchre weeping: and as she wept, she stooped down, and looked into the sepulchre, And seeth two angels in white sitting, the one at the head, and the other at the feet, where the body of Jesus had lain. And they say unto her, Woman, why weepest thou?

She saith unto them, Because they have taken away my Lord, and I know not where they have laid him.

And when she had thus said, she turned herself back, and saw Jesus standing, and knew not that it was Jesus. Jesus saith unto her, Woman, why weepest thou? whom seekest thou?

She, supposing him to be the gardener, saith unto him, Sir, if thou have borne him hence, tell me where thou hast laid him, and I will take him away.

Jesus saith unto her, Mary.

She turned herself, and saith unto him, Rabboni; which is to say, Master. Jesus saith unto her, Touch me not; for I am not yet ascended to my Father: but go to my brethren, and say unto them, I ascend unto my Father, and your Father; and to my God, and your God.

Mary Magdalene came and told the disciples that she had seen the Lord, and that he had spoken these things unto her. (John 20:11–18)

And she went and told them that had been with him, as they mourned and wept. And they, when they had heard that he was alive, and had been seen of her, believed not. (Mark 16:10–11)

---

*For ye have not received the spirit of bondage again to fear; but ye have received the Spirit of adoption, whereby we cry, Abba, Father. The Spirit itself beareth witness with our spirit, that we are the children of God. (Romans 8:15–16)*

HEIR OF SALVATION, PURCHASE OF GOD, BORN OF HIS SPIRIT, WASHED IN HIS BLOOD

# Be not afraid

It was Mary Magdalene and Joanna, and Mary the mother of James, and other women that were with them, which told these things unto the apostles.
(Luke 24:10)

And as they went to tell his disciples, behold, Jesus met them, saying, All hail. And they came and held him by the feet, and worshipped him. Then said Jesus unto them, Be not afraid: go tell my brethren that they go into Galilee, and there shall they see me.

   Now when they were going, behold, some of the watch came into the city, and shewed unto the chief priests all the things that were done. And when they were assembled with the elders, and had taken counsel, they gave large money unto the soldiers, Saying, Say ye, His disciples came by night, and stole him away while we slept. And if this come to the governor's ears, we will persuade him, and secure you. So they took the money, and did as they were taught: and this saying is commonly reported among the Jews until this day.
(Matthew 28:9–15)

---

*For the law made nothing perfect, but the bringing in of a better hope did; by the which we draw nigh unto God. And inasmuch as not without an oath he was made priest: (For those priests were made without an oath; but this with an oath by him that said unto him, The Lord sware and will not repent, Thou art a priest for ever after the order of Melchisedec:) By so much was Jesus made a surety of a better testament.*
*(Hebrews 7:19–22)*

# And their eyes were opened

And, behold, two of them went that same day to a village called Emmaus, which was from Jerusalem about threescore furlongs. And they talked together of all these things which had happened. And it came to pass, that, while they communed together and reasoned, Jesus himself drew near, and went with them. But their eyes were holden that they should not know him.

And he said unto them, What manner of communications are these that ye have one to another, as ye walk, and are sad?

And the one of them, whose name was Cleopas, answering said unto him, Art thou only a stranger in Jerusalem, and hast not known the things which are come to pass there in these days?

And he said unto them, What things?

And they said unto him, Concerning Jesus of Nazareth, which was a prophet mighty in deed and word before God and all the people: And how the chief priests and our rulers delivered him to be condemned to death, and have crucified him. But we trusted that it had been he which should have redeemed Israel: and beside all this, to day is the third day since these things were done. Yea, and certain women also of our company made us astonished, which were early at the sepulchre; And when they found not his body, they came, saying, that they had also seen a vision of angels, which said that he was alive. And certain of them which were with us went to the sepulchre, and found it even so as the women had said: but him they saw not.

Then he said unto them, O fools, and slow of heart to believe all that the prophets have spoken: Ought not Christ to have suffered these things, and to enter into his glory? And beginning at Moses and all the prophets, he expounded unto them in all the scriptures the things concerning himself.

And they drew nigh unto the village, whither they went: and he made as though he would have gone further. But they constrained him, saying, Abide with us: for it is toward evening, and the day is far spent. And he went in to tarry with them.

And it came to pass, as he sat at meat with them, he took bread, and blessed it, and brake, and gave to them. And their eyes were opened, and they knew him; and he vanished out of their sight.

And they said one to another, Did not our heart burn within us, while he talked with us by the way, and while he opened to us the scriptures? And they rose up the same hour, and returned to Jerusalem, and found the eleven gathered together, and them that were with them, Saying, The Lord is risen indeed, and hath appeared to Simon. And they told what things were done in the way, and how he was known of them in breaking of bread.
(Luke 24:13–35)

---

*But their minds were blinded: for until this day remaineth the same vail untaken away in the reading of the old testament; which vail is done away in Christ. But even unto this day, when Moses is read, the vail is upon their heart. Nevertheless when it shall turn to the Lord, the vail shall be taken away. Now the Lord is that Spirit: and where the Spirit of the Lord is, there is liberty.*
*(2 Corinthians 3:14–17)*

That the God of our Lord Jesus Christ, the
Father of glory, may give unto you the spirit of
wisdom and revelation in the knowledge of him:
The eyes of your understanding being enlightened;
that ye may know what is the hope of his calling,
and what the riches of the glory of his inheritance
in the saints, And what is the exceeding greatness
of his power to us-ward who believe, according
to the working of his mighty power, Which he
wrought in Christ, when he raised him from the
dead, and set him at his own right hand in the
heavenly places, Far above all principality, and
power, and might, and dominion, and every name
that is named, not only in this world, but also in
that which is to come: And hath put all things
under his feet, and gave him to be the head over
all things to the church, Which is his body, the
fulness of him that filleth all in all.

(Ephesians 1:17-23)

# Behold My hands and My feet, that it is I myself

And as they thus spake, Jesus himself stood in the midst of them, and saith unto them, Peace be unto you. But they were terrified and affrighted, and supposed that they had seen a spirit. And he said unto them, Why are ye troubled? and why do thoughts arise in your hearts? Behold my hands and my feet, that it is I myself: handle me, and see; for a spirit hath not flesh and bones, as ye see me have.

And when he had thus spoken, he shewed them his hands and his feet. And while they yet believed not for joy, and wondered, he said unto them, Have ye here any meat? And they gave him a piece of a broiled fish, and of an honeycomb. And he took it, and did eat before them.

And he said unto them, These are the words which I spake unto you, while I was yet with you, that all things must be fulfilled, which were written in the law of Moses, and in the prophets, and in the psalms, concerning me. Then opened he their understanding, that they might understand the scriptures,

And said unto them, Thus it is written, and thus it behooved Christ to suffer, and to rise from the dead the third day: And that repentance and remission of sins should be preached in his name among all nations, beginning at Jerusalem. And ye are witnesses of these things. And, behold, I send the promise of my Father upon you: but tarry ye in the city of Jerusalem, until ye be endued with power from on high.
(Luke 24:36–49)

---

*Therefore being justified by faith, we have peace with God through our Lord Jesus Christ: By whom also we have access by faith into this grace wherein we stand, and rejoice in hope of the glory of God.*
*(Romans 5:1–2)*

*Blessed be the God and Father of our Lord Jesus Christ, who hath blessed us with all spiritual blessings in heavenly places in Christ: According as he hath chosen us in him before the foundation of the world, that we should be holy and without blame before him in love: Having predestinated us unto the adoption of children by Jesus Christ to himself, according to the good pleasure of his will, To the praise of the glory of his grace, wherein he hath made us accepted in the beloved.*
*(Ephesians 1:3–6)*

There is therefore now no condemnation to them which are in Christ Jesus, who walk not after the flesh, but after the Spirit. For the law of the Spirit of life in Christ Jesus hath made me free from the law of sin and death. For what the law could not do, in that it was weak through the flesh, God sending his own Son in the likeness of sinful flesh, and for sin, condemned sin in the flesh: That the righteousness of the law might be fulfilled in us, who walk not after the flesh, but after the Spirit.

(Romans 8:1–4)

# Blessed are they that have not seen, and yet have believed

But Thomas, one of the twelve, called Didymus, was not with them when Jesus came. The other disciples therefore said unto him, We have seen the Lord.

But he said unto them, Except I shall see in his hands the print of the nails, and put my finger into the print of the nails, and thrust my hand into his side, I will not believe.

And after eight days again his disciples were within, and Thomas with them: then came Jesus, the doors being shut, and stood in the midst, and said, Peace be unto you. Then saith he to Thomas, Reach hither thy finger, and behold my hands; and reach hither thy hand, and thrust it into my side: and be not faithless, but believing.

And Thomas answered and said unto him, My Lord and my God.

Jesus saith unto him, Thomas, because thou hast seen me, thou hast believed: blessed are they that have not seen, and yet have believed.
(John 20:24–29)

---

*He that believeth on the Son of God hath the witness in himself: he that believeth not God hath made him a liar; because he believeth not the record that God gave of his Son. And this is the record, that God hath given to us eternal life, and this life is in his Son. He that hath the Son hath life; and he that hath not the Son of God hath not life. These things have I written unto you that believe on the name of the Son of God; that ye may know that ye have eternal life, and that ye may believe on the name of the Son of God.*
*(1 John 5:10–13)*

# Feed My sheep

After these things Jesus shewed himself again to the disciples at the sea of Tiberias; and on this wise shewed he himself. There were together Simon Peter, and Thomas called Didymus, and Nathanael of Cana in Galilee, and the sons of Zebedee, and two other of his disciples. Simon Peter saith unto them, I go a fishing.

They say unto him, We also go with thee. They went forth, and entered into a ship immediately; and that night they caught nothing. But when the morning was now come, Jesus stood on the shore: but the disciples knew not that it was Jesus. Then Jesus saith unto them, Children, have ye any meat?

They answered him, No.

And he said unto them, Cast the net on the right side of the ship, and ye shall find. They cast therefore, and now they were not able to draw it for the multitude of fishes.

Therefore that disciple whom Jesus loved saith unto Peter, It is the Lord. Now when Simon Peter heard that it was the Lord, he girt his fisher's coat unto him, (for he was naked,) and did cast himself into the sea. And the other disciples came in a little ship; (for they were not far from land, but as it were two hundred cubits,) dragging the net with fishes. As soon then as they were come to land, they saw a fire of coals there, and fish laid thereon, and bread. Jesus saith unto them, Bring of the fish which ye have now caught.

Simon Peter went up, and drew the net to land full of great fishes, an hundred and fifty and three: and for all there were so many, yet was not the net broken. Jesus saith unto them, Come and dine. And none of the disciples durst ask him, Who art thou? knowing that it was the Lord. Jesus then cometh, and taketh bread, and giveth them, and fish likewise.

This is now the third time that Jesus shewed himself to his disciples, after that he was risen from the dead.

So when they had dined, Jesus saith to Simon Peter, Simon, son of Jonas, lovest thou me more than these?

He saith unto him, Yea, Lord; thou knowest that I love thee.

He saith unto him, Feed my lambs.

He saith to him again the second time, Simon, son of Jonas, lovest thou me?

He saith unto him, Yea, Lord; thou knowest that I love thee. He saith unto him, Feed my sheep.

He saith unto him the third time, Simon, son of Jonas, lovest thou me? Peter was grieved because he said unto him the third time, Lovest thou me?

And he said unto him, Lord, thou knowest all things; thou knowest that I love thee.

Jesus saith unto him, Feed my sheep. Verily, verily, I say unto thee, When thou wast young, thou girdest thyself, and walkedst whither thou wouldest: but when thou shalt be old, thou shalt stretch forth thy hands, and another shall gird thee, and carry thee whither thou wouldest not. This spake he, signifying by what death he should glorify God. And when he had spoken this, he saith unto him, Follow me.

Then Peter, turning about, seeth the disciple whom Jesus loved following; which also leaned on his breast at supper, and said, Lord, which is he that betrayeth thee? Peter seeing him saith to Jesus, Lord, and what shall this man do?

Jesus saith unto him, If I will that he tarry till I come, what is that to thee? follow thou me.

Then went this saying abroad among the brethren, that that disciple should not die: yet Jesus said not unto him, He shall not die; but, If I will that he tarry till I come, what is that to thee?

This is the disciple which testifieth of these things, and wrote these things: and we know that his testimony is true.

And there are also many other things which Jesus did, the which, if they should be written every one, I suppose that even the world itself could not contain the books that should be written. Amen.
(John 21:1–25)

---

*Blessed be the God and Father of our Lord Jesus Christ, which according to his abundant mercy hath begotten us again unto a lively hope by the resurrection of Jesus Christ from the dead, To an inheritance incorruptible, and undefiled, and that fadeth not away, reserved in heaven for you, Who are kept by the power of God through faith unto salvation ready to be revealed in the last time.*
*(1 Peter 1:3–5)*

FORBID IT, LORD, THAT I SHOULD BOAST SAVE IN THE DEATH OF CHRIST, MY GOD

# According to the Scriptures

For I delivered unto you first of all that which I also received, how that Christ died for our sins according to the scriptures; And that he was buried, and that he rose again the third day according to the scriptures: And that he was seen of Cephas, then of the twelve: After that, he was seen of above five hundred brethren at once; of whom the greater part remain unto this present, but some are fallen asleep. After that, he was seen of James; then of all the apostles. And last of all he was seen of me also, as of one born out of due time.
(1 Corinthians 15:3–8)

---

*What shall we then say to these things? If God be for us, who can be against us? He that spared not his own Son, but delivered him up for us all, how shall he not with him also freely give us all things? Who shall lay any thing to the charge of God's elect? It is God that justifieth. Who is he that condemneth? It is Christ that died, yea rather, that is risen again, who is even at the right hand of God, who also maketh intercession for us. Who shall separate us from the love of Christ? shall tribulation, or distress, or persecution, or famine, or nakedness, or peril, or sword? As it is written, For thy sake we are killed all the day long; we are accounted as sheep for the slaughter. Nay, in all these things we are more than conquerors through him that loved us.*
*(Romans 8:31–37)*

WHO YIELDED HIS LIFE AN ATONEMENT FOR SIN, AND OPENED THE LIFE GATE THAT WE MAY GO IN

For I am persuaded, that neither death, nor life, nor angels, nor principalities, nor powers, nor things present, nor things to come, Nor height, nor depth, nor any other creature, shall be able to separate us from the love of God, which is in Christ Jesus our Lord.

(Romans 8:38–39)

# I am with you always, even unto the end of the world

Then the eleven disciples went away into Galilee, into a mountain where Jesus had appointed them. And when they saw him, they worshipped him: but some doubted.

And Jesus came and spake unto them, saying, All power is given unto me in heaven and in earth. Go ye therefore, and teach all nations, baptizing them in the name of the Father, and of the Son, and of the Holy Ghost: Teaching them to observe all things whatsoever I have commanded you: and, lo, I am with you always, even unto the end of the world. Amen. (Matthew 28:16–20)

And these signs shall follow them that believe; In my name shall they cast out devils; they shall speak with new tongues; They shall take up serpents; and if they drink any deadly thing, it shall not hurt them; they shall lay hands on the sick, and they shall recover. (Mark 16:17–18)

And, being assembled together with them, commanded them that they should not depart from Jerusalem, but wait for the promise of the Father, which, saith he, ye have heard of me. For John truly baptized with water; but ye shall be baptized with the Holy Ghost not many days hence.

When they therefore were come together, they asked of him, saying, Lord, wilt thou at this time restore again the kingdom to Israel? And he said unto them, It is not for you to know the times or the seasons, which the Father hath put in his own power. But ye shall receive power, after that the Holy Ghost is come upon you: and ye shall be witnesses unto me both in Jerusalem, and in all Judaea, and in Samaria, and unto the uttermost part of the earth.

And when he had spoken these things, while they beheld, he was taken up; and a cloud received him out of their sight. And while they looked stedfastly toward heaven as he went up, behold, two men stood by them in white apparel; Which also said, Ye men of Galilee, why stand ye gazing up into heaven? this same Jesus, which is taken up from you into heaven, shall so come in like manner as ye have seen him go into heaven. (Acts 1:4–11)

So then after the Lord had spoken unto them, he was received up into heaven, and sat on the right hand of God. And they went forth, and preached every where, the Lord working with them, and confirming the word with signs following. Amen. (Mark 16:19–20)

---

*For I would not, brethren, that ye should be ignorant of this mystery, lest ye should be wise in your own conceits; that blindness in part is happened to Israel, until the fulness of the Gentiles be come in. And so all Israel shall be saved: as it is written, There shall come out of Sion the Deliverer, and shall turn away ungodliness from Jacob: For this is my covenant unto them, when I shall take away their sins. (Romans 11:25–27)*

*Having therefore, brethren, boldness to enter into the holiest by the blood of Jesus, By a new and living way, which he hath consecrated for us, through the veil, that is to say, his flesh; And having an high priest over the house of God; Let us draw near with a true heart in full assurance of faith, having our hearts sprinkled from an evil conscience, and our bodies washed with pure water. Let us hold fast the profession of our faith without wavering; (for he is faithful that promised). (Hebrews 10:19–23)*

And, behold, I come quickly; and my reward is with me, to give every man according as his work shall be. I am Alpha and Omega, the beginning and the end, the first and the last. Blessed are they that do his commandments, that they may have right to the tree of life, and may enter in through the gates into the city.
(Revelation 22:12–14)

*For Christ is not entered into the holy places made with hands, which are the figures of the true; but into heaven itself, now to appear in the presence of God for us.*
*(Hebrews 9:24)*

*And let us consider one another to provoke unto love and to good works: Not forsaking the assembling of ourselves together, as the manner of some is; but exhorting one another: and so much the more, as ye see the day approaching.*
*(Hebrews 10:24–25)*

*He which testifieth these things saith, Surely I come quickly. Amen. Even so, come, Lord Jesus. The grace of our Lord Jesus Christ be with you all. Amen.*
*(Revelation 22:20–21)*

O FOR A THOUSAND TONGUES TO SING. MY GREAT REDEEMER'S PRAISE, THE GLORIES OF MY GOD AND KING, THE TRIUMPHS OF HIS GRACE

# Acknowledgements

HYMNS

And can it be that I should gain (Charles Wesley, 1738)   Guide me, O Thou great Jehovah (William Williams, 1745) (translated by Peter Williams, 1771)   Praise God, from Whom all blessings flow (Thomas Ken, 1674)   The first Nowell, the angel did say (Unknown, 1833)   O Holy night (Placide Cappeau, 1847) (Translated by John S. Dwight, 1855)   In His temple now behold Him (Henry J. Pye, 1851)   O little town of Bethlehem (Phillips Brooks, 1868) O come, all ye faithful (attributed to John Francis Wade, 1751) (translated by Frederick Oakeley, 1852)   This is my Father's world (Maltbie D. Babcock, 1901)   The love of God is greater far (Frederick M. Lehman, 1917)   What a friend we have in Jesus, all our sins and griefs to bear (Joseph Medlicott Scriven, 1855)   Rock of Ages, cleft for me (Augustus Toplady, 1776)   Come, sinners, to the gospel feast (Charles Wesley, 1747)   Holy, holy, holy! Lord God almighty! (Reginald Heber, 1826)   Holy Spirit, truth divine, dawn upon this soul of mine (Samuel Longfellow, 1864) Be thou my vision, O Lord of my heart (attributed to Dallán Forgaill) (translated by Eleanor H. Hull, 1905)   Come, thou fount of every blessing (Robert Robinson, 1758)   Jesus paid it all (Elvina M. Hall, 1865)   Be still, my soul: the Lord is on thy side (Kathrina von Schlegel, 1752) (translated by Jane Borthwick, 1855)   O for a thousand tongues to sing (Charles Wesley, 1739)   My hope is built on nothing less (Edward Mote, 1834)   Take my life and let it be (Frances Ridley Havergal, 1874)   Amazing grace! How sweet the sound (John Newton, 1779)   Pass me not, O gentle Saviour (Fanny Crosby, 1868)   Turn your eyes upon Jesus (Helen Howarth Lemmel, 1922)  Fairest Lord Jesus (Unknown, 1677)   O scatter seeds of loving deeds (Jessie Brown Pounds, 1887)   Open my eyes, that I may see (Clara H. Scott, 1895)   Great is thy faithfulness, O God my Father (Thomas O. Chisholm, 1923)   We have an anchor (Priscilla J. Owens, 1882)   Break thou the bread of life (Mary A. Lathbury, 1877)   I know not why God's wondrous grace to me he hath made known (D. W. Whittle, 1883)   God will take care of you (Civilla D. Martin, 1904)   O give thanks unto the Lord, give thanks (Eliza E. Hewitt, 1892)   Sweet hour of prayer (William W. Walford, 1845) Saviour, like a shepherd lead us (Attributed to Dorothy A. Thrupp, 1836)   I stand amazed in the presence (Chas. H. Gabriel, 1905)   Love Lifted Me (James Rowe, 1912)  Leaning on the everlasting arms (E. A. Hoffman, 1887)   'Tis so sweet to trust in Jesus (Louisa M. R. Stead, 1882)  All to Jesus I surrender (Judson W. Van De Venter, 1896)   Bread of the world, in mercy broken (Reginald Heber, 1827)  Depth of mercy! Can there be (Charles Wesley, 1740)   There is a fountain filled with blood drawn from Emmanuel's veins (William Cowper, 1772)   When I survey the wondrous cross (Isaac Watts, 1707)   Here is love as vast as the ocean (William Rees, William Williams, William Edwards, 1900) Christ arose (Robert Lowry, 1874)   To God be the glory, great things he hath done (Fanny Crosby, 1875)   Blessed assurance (Frances J. Crosby, 1873)   Crown Him with many crowns (Matthew Bridges, 1851)

*No condemnation now I dread; Jesus, and all in Him is mine!*
*Alive in Him, my living Head, And clothed in righteousness divine,*
*Bold I approach th'eternal throne, And claim the crown, through Christ my own*
*("And Can It Be" by Charles Wesley, 1738)*

# About the illustrator

Dominic Fam is an illustrator based in Singapore. His main body of work is in branding and advertising, and his illustrations have appeared in numerous ad campaigns, FMCG materials, multimedia and many other projects. He works in a variety of illustration styles from digital photorealistic renderings to traditional art such as pen/ink/paint media. His background includes photography, graphic and web design.

Intrigued and inspired by the paintings and sculptures he grew up seeing in church, he has been drawing Bible characters since he was a child. His fascination with Christian art has continued well into his professional life, as he continued experimenting with new artistic styles and methods to create his Bible-themed illustrations during his spare time.

The selection of artwork in this book (originally produced as large format digital paintings) was created roughly from 2006 to 2019, whenever he was in between commercial projects.